Workshop on the Relevance of Linguistic Structure in Neural Architectures for NLP 2018

Held at ACL 2018

Melbourne, Australia
19 July 2018

ISBN: 978-1-5108-6716-1

Printed from e-media with permission by:

Curran Associates, Inc.
57 Morehouse Lane
Red Hook, NY 12571

Printed by Curran Associates, Inc. (2018)

For permission requests, please contact the Association for Computational Linguistics at the address below.

Association for Computational Linguistics
209 N. Eighth Street
Stroudsburg, Pennsylvania 18360

Phone: 1-570-476-8006
Fax: 1-570-476-0860

acl@aclweb.org

Additional copies of this publication are available from:

Curran Associates, Inc.
57 Morehouse Lane
Red Hook, NY 12571 USA
Phone: 845-758-0400
Fax: 845-758-2633
Email: curran@proceedings.com
Web: www.proceedings.com

ACL 2018

Relevance of Linguistic Structure in Neural Architectures for NLP

Proceedings of the Workshop

July 19, 2018
Melbourne, Australia

Preface

Welcome to the ACL Workshop on the Relevance of Linguistic Structure in Neural Architectures for NLP (RELNLP). The workshop took place on July 19th 2018, collocated with the 56th Annual Meeting of the Association for Computational Linguistics in Melbourne, Australia.

There is a long standing tradition in NLP focusing on fundamental language modeling tasks such as morphological analysis, POS tagging, parsing, WSD or semantic parsing. In the context of end-user NLP tasks, these have played the role of enabling technologies, providing a layer of representation upon which more complex tasks can be built. However, in recent years we have witnessed a number of success stories involving end-to-end architectures trained on large data and making little or no use of a linguistically-informed language representation layer. This workshop's focus was on the role of linguistic structures in the neural network era. We aimed to gauge their significance in building better, more generalizable NLP.

The workshop has accepted 2 oral presentations and a total of 7 poster presentations. The program also included four invited speakers as well as a panel discussion. We would like to thank our speakers: Chris Dyer, Emily Bender, Jason Eisner and Mark Johnson as well as our program committee for their work in assuring high quality and on time reviews.

Georgiana Dinu, Miguel Ballesteros, Avirup Sil, Sam Bowman, Wael Hamza, Anders Søgaard, Tahira Naseem and Yoav Goldberg

Organizers:

Georgiana Dinu, Amazon AWS
Miguel Ballesteros, IBM Research
Avirup Sil, IBM Research
Sam Bowman, NYU
Wael Hamza, Amazon Alexa
Anders Søgaard, University of Copenhagen
Tahira Naseem, IBM Research
Yoav Goldberg, Bar Ilan University

Program Committee:

Eneko Agirre, Basque Country University, Spain
Yonatan Belinkov, CSAIL, MIT, USA
Jose Camacho-Collados, Sapienza-Universty of Rome, Italy
Xavier Carreras, Naver Labs Europe, France
Ryan Cotterell, Johns Hopkins University, USA
Jacob Eisenstein, Georgia Institute of Technology, USA
Jason Eisner, Johns Hopkins University, USA
Katrin Erk, University of Texas at Austin, USA
Luis Espinosa-Anke, Cardiff University, UK
Manaal Faruqui, Google Research, USA
Orhan Firat, Google Research, USA
Markus Freitag, Google Research, USA
Ramón Fernández-Astudillo, Unbabel, Portugal
Matt Gardner, Allen Institute for Artificial Intelligence, USA
Carlos Gómez-Rodrígez, University of A Coruña, Spain
Benjamin Han, Microsoft AI + R, USA
Douwe Kiela, FAIR, USA
Eliyahu Kiperwasser, Bar-Illan University, Israel
Adhiguna Kuncoro, Deepmind and University of Oxford, UK
Sandra Kübler, Indiana University, USA
Mirella Lapata, University of Edinburgh, UK
Tao Lei, ASAPP, New York, NY
Roger Levy, MIT, USA
Haitao Mi, Ant Financial, USA
Maria Nadejde, University of Edinburgh, UK
Ramesh Nallapati, Amazon, USA
Karthik Narasimhan, Open AI, USA
Joakim Nivre, Uppsala University, Sweden
Barbara Plank, University of Groeningen, Netherlands
Tamara Polajnar, Cambridge University/Mrs. Wordsmith, UK
Alessandro Raganato, Sapienza-Universty of Rome, Italy
Sebastian Ruder, Insight Research Centre for Data Analytics, Ireland
Alexander Rush, Harvard University, USA
Karl Stratos, Toyota Technological Institute at Chicago, USA
Sara Stymme, Uppsala University, Sweden

Yulia Tsetkov, Carnegie Mellon University, USA
Eva Maria Vecchi, University of Stuttgart, Germany
Adina Williams, NYU, USA
Bing Xiang, Amazon AWS, USA

Invited Speakers:

Chris Dyer, DeepMind, Carnegie Mellon University
Emily Bender, University of Washington
Jason Eisner, Johns Hopkins University
Mark Johnson, Macquarie University

Table of Contents

Conference Program

Thursday, June 19, 2018

8:50–9:00 *Opening Remarks*

Session 1

9:00–10:00 *Invited Talk: Chris Dyer*

10:00–10:20 *Compositional Morpheme Embeddings with Affixes as Functions and Stems as Arguments*
Daniel Edmiston and Karl Stratos

10:20–11:00 *Break*

Session 2

11:00–12:00 *Invited Talk: Mark Johnson*

12:00–12:20 *Unsupervised Source Hierarchies for Low-Resource Neural Machine Translation*
Anna Currey and Kenneth Heafield

12:20–13:30 *Lunch*

Session 3

13:30–14:30 *Poster session*

14:30–15:30 *Invited Talk: Jason Eisner*

15:30–16:00 *Break*

Session 4

16:00–17:00 *Invited Talk: Emily Bender*

17:00–18:00 *Panel discussion*

Compositional Morpheme Embeddings with Affixes as Functions and Stems as Arguments

Daniel Edmiston
University of Chicago
danedmiston@uchicago.edu

Karl Stratos
Toyota Technical Institute at Chicago
stratos@ttic.edu

Abstract

This work introduces a linguistically motivated architecture, which we label STAFFNET, for composing morphemes to derive word embeddings. The principal novelty in the work is to treat stems as vectors and affixes as functions over vectors. In this way, our model's architecture more closely resembles the compositionality of morphemes in natural language. Such a model stands in opposition to models which treat morphemes uniformly, making no distinction between stem and affix. We run this new architecture on a dependency parsing task in Korean—a language rich in derivational morphology—and compare it against a lexical baseline, along with other sub-word architectures. STAFFNET shows competitive performance with the state-of-the-art on this task.

1 Introduction

This work proposes a novel architecture for the composition of morphemes to derive word embeddings. The architecture is motivated by linguistic considerations and is designed to mirror the composition of morphemes in natural language. This means making a hard distinction between affix and stem (e.g. between content morphemes like stem *dog* and functional morphemes like plural affix *-s* in the word *dogs*), and recognizing the function-argument relation between them. We reflect this in our architecture by treating stems as vectors in $\mathbb{R}^n$, and affixes as functions (either linear or non-linear, depending on model) from $\mathbb{R}^n$ to $\mathbb{R}^n$. Given the importance of stems and affixes in the architecture, we label it St(em)Aff(ix)Net.

We test the viability of the linguistically motivated STAFFNET on a dependency parsing task in Korean—a language rich in derivational morphology. Here, we achieve promising results for infusing explicit linguistic analyses into NLP architectures. Specifically, the architecture achieves results which significantly outperform simple word-embedding baselines, and are competitive with other sub-word architectures which constitute the current state-of-the-art for this task in Korean (Stratos, 2017).

We therefore submit the following as our contributions:

- We introduce a novel architecture for the composition of word-embeddings which is explicitly designed to mirror composition of morphologically complex words in natural language.
- Our novel architecture achieves state-of-the-art performance in every case (see Table 1), suggesting linguistic structure can be viable for real-world NLP tasks.

2 Related Work

This work falls under a large body of work on incorporating linguistically sound structures into neural networks for more effective text representation. One such line of work is sub-lexical models. In these models, word representations are enriched by explicitly modeling characters (Ma and Hovy, 2016; Kim et al., 2016) or morphemes (Luong et al., 2013; Botha and Blunsom, 2014; Cotterell et al., 2016). For languages with complex orthography, sub-*character* models have also been proposed. Previous works consider modeling graphical components of Chinese characters called radicals (Sun et al., 2014; Yin et al., 2016) and syllable-blocks of Korean characters—either

Proceedings of the Workshop on the Relevance of Linguistic Structure in Neural Architectures for NLP, pages 1–5
Melbourne, Australia, July 19, 2018. ©2018 Association for Computational Linguistics

as atomic (Choi et al., 2017) or as non-linear functions of underlying *jamo* letters through Unicode decomposition (Stratos, 2017).

The present work also aims to incorporate subword information into word embeddings, and does so by modeling morphology. However, this work differs from those above in the means of composition, as our method is based principally on function application. Here, we take derivational morphemes (i.e. affixes) as functions, and stems as arguments. Broadly speaking, this work can be seen as an extension of Baroni et al. (2014)'s compositional distributional semantic framework to the sub-word level. At a more narrow level, our work is reminiscent of Baroni and Zamparelli (2010), who model adjectives as matrices and nouns as vectors, and work like Hartung et al. (2017), which seeks to learn composition functions in addition to vector representations.

3 Architecture and Linguistic Motivation

The intuition behind the decision to treat stems and affixes differently is that to do otherwise is to miss a key linguistic generalization with regard to the composition of complex words. Furthermore, we argue that to include stems and affixes in the same space for comparison is akin to doing the same for, say, real numbers and functions over real numbers. In the same way that the squaring operation is defined as a function of its input, we argue that an affix has meaning only insofar as the effect it produces on its stem.

Regarding the behavior of morpheme composition in natural language, we know that stems can compose to form compounds, and affixes can attach successively to a stem. However, affixes cannot exist in isolation—they must attach to a stem. We seek for our architecture to display each of these properties: compounding, successive affix attachment, and inability to represent an affix on its own. Therefore, in order to induce compositional morpheme representations, we learn not only vectors for stems, but also a weight matrix and bias for each affix.

To accomplish this, we use the *Komoran* part-of-speech tagger included in the *KoNLPy*[1] toolkit, and have a trained theoretical linguist separate out the stem parts of speech from the affix parts of speech. We then parse Korean words into constituent stems and affixes, and compute the com-

[1]Documentation for which is available at `konlpy.org`.

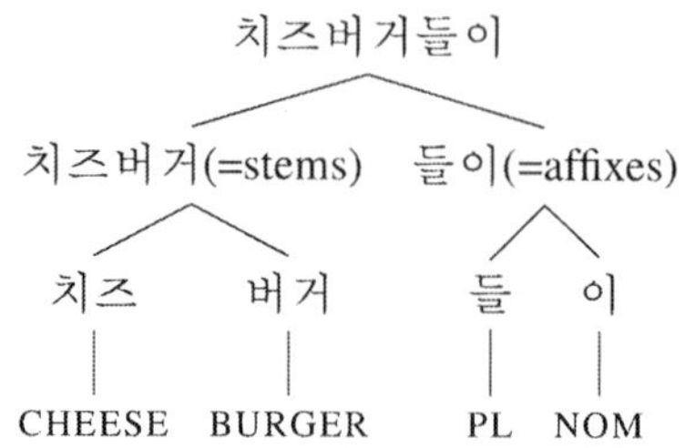

Figure 1: Decomposition of 치즈버거들이 (=*cheese.burger*-PL.NOM)

positional representation of a word from these constituent parts using a dynamic neural-network architecture. The architecture can be conceptually broken into three steps: (i) decomposing the word into its constituent stems and affixes, (ii) computing the composite stem representation, and then (iii) iteratively applying (equivalent to function composition) the affix functions over the stem representation.

To illustrate how the architecture works in detail, we consider the morphologically complex Korean word for "*cheeseburgers*" marked with nominative case: 치즈버거들이(=*cheese.burger*-PL.NOM).

First, the word is decomposed by our part-of-speech tagger into a list of stems, [*cheese*, *burger*], and a list of affixes, [PL, NOM]. This decomposition is as in Figure 1. Given a list of stems, we decide how to construct a stem representation made from the elements in that list. If the stem list has only a single member, we simply return that stem's representation as the full stem representation.

Since *cheese.burger* is a compound stem, we must go through the step of constructing a composite stem representation. To do this, we first run a vanilla bi-directional RNN over the stem sequence (the choice of a vanilla BiRNN rather than a more powerful mechanism capable of capturing long distance dependencies rests on the apparent fact that Korean morphological dependencies are strictly local, lacking phenomena like circumfixes or non-concatenative morphology). This produces an intermediate output for each stem in the sequence, $e^{<t>}$, which we weight and then sum together for the composite stem representation.

In order to calculate the proper weighting for each stem, $w^{<t>}$, we compare each output of the RNN via cosine-similarity with a pre-trained embedding of the full sequence of stems, in this case 치 즈 버 거, or *cheeseburger* with no affixes attached.[2] This gives us scores $s^{<1>} = cos(cheeseburger, cheese)$ and $s^{<2>} = cos(cheeseburger, burger)$. We softmax the sequence $[s^{<1>}, s^{<2>}]$, giving us our weights $w^{<1>}$ and $w^{<2>}$. The composite stem representation is then the sum of our weighted intermediate scores, i.e. $\sum_t w^{<t>} \cdot e^{<t>}$.

Presumably, since the word *cheeseburger* acts more like *burger* than *cheese*, *burger* will receive a higher cosine similarity and thus be weighted more. In this way, our system has a natural and dynamic way of weighting stems.

Now that we have a composite stem representation, we can feed it iteratively as an argument to the affix list. Here, each affix is represented either as a non-linear function $\lambda x.tanh(W \cdot x + b)$ in the model we call STAFFNET NON-LINEAR, or as a linear function $\lambda x.W \cdot x + b$ in the model we call STAFFNET LINEAR (though there is still non-linearity in the RNN calculating the composite stem representations). The models are otherwise identical, and in each case W and b are learnable parameters. The STAFFNET NON-LINEAR computation graph for the example 치즈버거들이(= *cheese.burger*-PL.NOM), or *cheeseburgers* in the nominative case, is as in Figure 2.

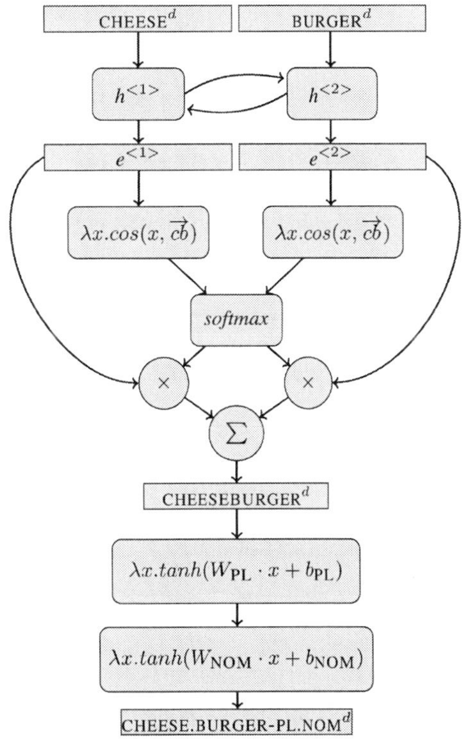

Figure 2: Composition of complex word *cheese.burger*-PL.NOM

4 Performance on Parsing Task

In order to test the efficacy of our composition method, we ran experiments for both our linear and non-linear models on a dependency parsing task using a publicly available Korean treebank (McDonald et al., 2013).[3] Word vectors were composed as described above in 100 dimensions, and then these representations were inserted into the BiLSTM model of Kiperwasser and Goldberg (2016).[4] We then compared our results to the original results in McDonald et al. (2013) and to those reported in Stratos (2017) for various sub-word architectures also run with Kiperwasser & Goldberg's parser. These results were all trained on a training set of 5,425 sentences over 30 epochs, with the best model being chosen from a dev set of 603 sentences. Finally, the test set consisted of 298 examples. The results are summarized in Table 1.

System	embedding	UAS	LAS
McDonald13	word	71.22	55.85
K&G16	word	90.00	82.77
Stratos17	syllable	94.75	90.81
	letter	94.59	90.77
	syllable/letter	94.79	91.19
	word/syl/let	95.17	92.31
STAFFNET NON-LINEAR	stem & affix	95.17	92.89
	word/stem & affix	95.06	92.93
STAFFNET LINEAR	stem & affix	**95.48**	**93.43**
	word/stem & affix	95.17	93.32

Table 1: System comparison

A quick examination of Table 1 shows that our systems significantly outperform lexical baselines, showing that the incorporation of sub-word information in a linguistically motivated fashion can demonstrate good performance on NLP tasks. Furthermore, our models are highly competitive with competing sub-word architectures. Both STAFFNET models achieve virtually identical results with those in Stratos (2017), with the STAFFNET LINEAR model slightly edging out the others. It is perhaps surprising that neither the

[2]The pre-trained embeddings are *word2vec* (Mikolov et al., 2013), skip-gram-induced embeddings with a window of 5.

[3]https://github.com/ryanmcd/uni-dep-tb

[4]https://github.com/elikip/bist-parser

addition of non-linearity to affix transformations, nor the concatenation of lexical representations to STAFFNET representations appear to make any significant change in results.

It is worth noting that the jump provided by incorporating sub-word information is significantly higher for LAS than UAS when compared to the lexical baselines.[5] This could be due to the simple fact that there is more room for improvement in LAS than UAS, but we speculate below on a potentially more interesting explanation based on the apparent role of (certain types of) morphology in natural language.

5 Discussion

It is no surprise that incorporating sub-word information outperforms more basic, lexically tokenized systems, and given the results in Table 1, it is easy to be optimistic with regard to the idea of incorporating sub-word information in a linguistically motivated fashion.

But what's interesting is not so much the fact that STAFFNET outperformed lexical baselines, it is how it did it. In the best case, STAFFNET outperformed K&G's BiLSTM model with simple word embeddings by 5.48 in UAS, but by 10.66 in LAS. We hypothesize that this jump was not simply due to there being more room for improvement in LAS. Rather, we speculate that this significant improvement in LAS was due to the apparent role of certain types of morphology in natural language, particularly case morphology. The role of case morphology in natural language is to mark relations between syntactic constituents. An explicit marker for syntactic relations like case morphology is likely to aid in a task like LAS, where the goal is to label these syntactic relationships. This is especially true for Korean, where case morphology is both regular and frequent. We hypothesize that morphologically aware architectures like STAFFNET are well suited to leverage this information when labelling arcs.

It may be asked why the syllable-based embeddings of Stratos (2017) also showed such a strong improvement over lexical baselines in LAS versus UAS (82.77 to 90.81 and 90.00 to 94.75), but this may have to do with the nature of the lexical makeup of the Korean language. The vocabulary of the Korean language is, depending on dictionary, made up of between 52% and 69% of words of Chinese origin, known as *hanja*. These *hanja* are single-syllable, meaning-bearing units, meaning it's very likely that syllable embeddings implicitly capture a great deal of meaningful lexical content in a way that similar sub-word architectures (e.g. *fastText*; Bojanowski et al., 2016) in languages like English cannot. Furthermore, many of the most common case-markings in Korean consist of a lone syllable, meaning this system too would have a strong advantage at implicitly capturing case meaning, and therefore have an advantage when labelling arcs. It is less clear what to make of the effectiveness of compositional letter embeddings for Korean, though this representation has by far the smallest number of parameters and yet still shows state-of-the-art performance, making it the most practical choice of sub-word architecture for Korean.

6 Conclusion and Future Work

This paper introduced a novel architecture, STAFFNET, for composing word embeddings using morphemes as atomic units. It was novel in that it made a distinction between stem representations and affix representations, the former being vectors and the latter being (non-)linear functions over those vectors. The intuition is to more closely mimic how natural language is thought to handle morphological composition and make a distinction between the lexically contentful and the functional. We tested the mettle of this architecture in a dependency parsing task, where it showed very strong results, slightly outperforming the state-of-the-art.

In addition to the practical import of achieving state-of-the-art performance in a novel way, we argue that this exercise has been both useful and enlightening from a linguistic viewpoint. Useful in that a linguistically motivated system shows strong performance and emerges as a candidate for sub-word architectures (at least in morphologically rich languages like Korean), and enlightening in that the manner in which these compositional morphemes improve upon the lexical baseline is disproportionate in helping the parser label its arcs. We speculate that this is because the nature of relations between syntactic entities is often reflected in the morphology, and this is especially

[5]Labeled Attachment Score, or LAS, refers to the percentage of correct assignments of words to their heads along with the correct label. Unlabaled Attachment Score, or UAS, refers only to the percentage of correct attachments, regardless of label.

true in languages rich in case morphology.

We see future work going forward in any of three directions:

- Improving upon the system described here; we rely on the *Komoran* part-of-speech tagger for decomposing words—is there a better way to do this? Was the choice of vanilla BiRNN for composite stem representation a good one? Could we achieve even higher results with more sophisticated networks?
- Testing this architecture on other languages. Korean is rich in case morphology. Would our system show such improvement over lexical baselines on languages with more impoverished morphology?
- Can this type of architecture be successful at the level of syntax, as a means of deriving compositional sentence embeddings?

Acknowledgments

The authors would like to thank John Goldsmith and Liwen Zhang for stimulating discussion related to STAFFNET.

References

Marco Baroni, Raffaella Bernardi, and Roberto Zamparelli. 2014. Frege in space: A program for compositional distributional semantics. Linguistic Issues in Language Technology, 9:241–346.

Marco Baroni and Roberto Zamparelli. 2010. Nouns are vectors, adjectives are matrices: Representing adjective-noun constructions in semantic space. In Proceedings of the 2010 Conference on Empirical Methods in Natural Language Processing, pages 1183–1193.

Piotr Bojanowski, Edouard Grave, Armand Joulin, and Tomas Mikolov. 2016. Enriching word vectors with subword information.

Jan A Botha and Phil Blunsom. 2014. Compositional morphology for word representations and language modelling. In ICML, pages 1899–1907.

Sanghyuk Choi, Taeuk Kim, Jinseok Seol, and Sanggoo Lee. 2017. A syllable-based technique for word embeddings of Korean words. In Proceedings of the First Workshop on Subword and Character Level Models in NLP, pages 36–40.

Ryan Cotterell, Hinrich Schütze, and Jason Eisner. 2016. Morphological smoothing and extrapolation of word embeddings. In Proceedings of the 54th Annual Meeting of the Association for Computational Linguistics, volume 1, pages 1651–1660.

Matthias Hartung, Fabian Kaupmann, Soufian Jebbara, and Philipp Cimiano. 2017. Learning compositionality functions on word embeddings for modelling attribute meaning in adjective-noun phrases. In Proceedings of the 15th Conference of the European Chapter of the Association for Computational Linguistics, volume 1, pages 54–64.

Yoon Kim, Yacine Jernite, David Sontag, and Alexander M Rush. 2016. Character-aware neural language models. In Thirtieth AAAI Conference on Artificial Intelligence.

Eliyahu Kiperwasser and Yoav Goldberg. 2016. Simple and accurate dependency parsing using bidirectional lstm feature representations. In Transactions of the Association for Computational Linguistics, volume 4, pages 313–327.

Thang Luong, Richard Socher, and Christopher D Manning. 2013. Better word representations with recursive neural networks for morphology. In CoNLL, pages 104–113.

Xuezhe Ma and Eduard Hovy. 2016. End-to-end sequence labeling via bi-directional lstm-cnns-crf. In Proceedings of the 54th Annual Meeting of the Association for Computational Linguistics (Volume 1: Long Papers), pages 1064 1074, Berlin, Germany. Association for Computational Linguistics.

Ryan McDonald, Joakim Nivre, Yvonne Quirmbach-Brundage, Yoav Goldberg, Dipanjan Das, Kuzman Ganchev, Keith Hall, Slav Petrov, Hao Zhang, Oscar Täckström, Claudia Bedini, Núria Bertomeu Castelló, and Jungmee Lee. 2013. Universal dependency annotation for multilingual parsing. In Proceedings of the 51st Annual Meeting of the Association for Computational Linguistics, volume 2, pages 92–97.

Tomas Mikolov, Ilya Sutskever, Kai Chen, Greg Corrado, and Jeff Dean. 2013. Distributed representations of words and phrases and their compositionality. In Advances in neural information processing systems, pages 3111–3119.

Karl Stratos. 2017. A sub-character architecture for Korean language processing. In Proceedings of the 2017 Conference on Empirical Methods in Natural Language Processing, pages 721–726, Copenhagen, Denmark. Association for Computational Linguistics.

Yaming Sun, Lei Lin, Nan Yang, Zhenzhou Ji, and Xiaolong Wang. 2014. Radical-enhanced Chinese character embedding. In International Conference on Neural Information Processing, pages 279–286. Springer.

Rongchao Yin, Quan Wang, Rui Li, Peng Li, and Bin Wang. 2016. Multi-granularity Chinese word embedding. In Proceedings of the Empiricial Methods in Natural Language Processing.

Unsupervised Source Hierarchies for Low-Resource Neural Machine Translation

Anna Currey
University of Edinburgh
a.currey@sms.ed.ac.uk

Kenneth Heafield
University of Edinburgh
kheafiel@inf.ed.ac.uk

Abstract

Incorporating source syntactic information into neural machine translation (NMT) has recently proven successful (Eriguchi et al., 2016; Luong et al., 2016). However, this is generally done using an outside parser to syntactically annotate the training data, making this technique difficult to use for languages or domains for which a reliable parser is not available. In this paper, we introduce an unsupervised tree-to-sequence (tree2seq) model for neural machine translation; this model is able to induce an unsupervised hierarchical structure on the source sentence based on the downstream task of neural machine translation. We adapt the Gumbel tree-LSTM of Choi et al. (2018) to NMT in order to create the encoder.

We evaluate our model against sequential and supervised parsing baselines on three low- and medium-resource language pairs. For low-resource cases, the unsupervised tree2seq encoder significantly outperforms the baselines; no improvements are seen for medium-resource translation.

1 Introduction

Neural machine translation (NMT) is a widely used approach to machine translation that is often trained without outside linguistic information. In NMT, sentences are typically modeled using recurrent neural networks (RNNs), so they are represented in a continuous space, alleviating the sparsity issue that afflicted many previous machine translation approaches. As a result, NMT is state-of-the-art for many language pairs (Bentivogli et al., 2016; Toral and Sánchez-Cartagena, 2017).

Despite these successes, there is room for improvement. RNN-based NMT is sequential, whereas natural language is hierarchical; thus, RNNs may not be the most appropriate models for language. In fact, these sequential models do not fully learn syntax (Bentivogli et al., 2016; Linzen et al., 2016; Shi et al., 2016). In addition, although NMT performs well on high-resource languages, it is less successful in low-resource scenarios (Koehn and Knowles, 2017).

As a solution to these challenges, researchers have incorporated syntax into NMT, particularly on the source side. Notably, Eriguchi et al. (2016) introduced a tree-to-sequence (tree2seq) NMT model in which the RNN encoder was augmented with a tree long short-term memory (LSTM) network (Tai et al., 2015). This and related techniques have yielded improvements in NMT; however, injecting source syntax into NMT requires parsing the training data with an external parser, and such parsers may be unavailable for low-resource languages. Adding syntactic source information may improve low-resource NMT, but we would need a way of doing so without an external parser.

We would like to mimic the improvements that come from adding source syntactic hierarchies to NMT without requiring syntactic annotations of the training data. Recently, there have been some proposals to induce unsupervised hierarchies based on semantic objectives for sentiment analysis and natural language inference (Choi et al., 2018; Yogatama et al., 2017). Here, we apply these hierarchical sentence representations to low-resource neural machine translation.

In this work, we adapt the Gumbel tree-LSTM of Choi et al. (2018) to low-resource NMT, allowing unsupervised hierarchies to be injected into the encoder. We compare this model to sequential neural machine translation, as well as to NMT enriched with information from an external parser.

Proceedings of the Workshop on the Relevance of Linguistic Structure in Neural Architectures for NLP, pages 6–12
Melbourne, Australia, July 19, 2018.

Our proposed model yields significant improvements in very low-resource NMT without requiring outside data or parsers beyond what is used in standard NMT; in addition, this model is not significantly slower to train than RNN-based models.

2 Neural Machine Translation

Neural machine translation (Cho et al., 2014; Kalchbrenner and Blunsom, 2013; Sutskever et al., 2014) is an end-to-end neural approach to machine translation consisting of an encoder, a decoder, and an attention mechanism (Bahdanau et al., 2015). The encoder and decoder are usually LSTMs (Hochreiter and Schmidhuber, 1997) or gated recurrent units (GRUs) (Cho et al., 2014). The encoder reads in the source sentence and creates an embedding; the attention mechanism calculates a weighted combination of the words in the source sentence. This is then fed into the decoder, which uses the source representations to generate a translation in the target language.

3 Unsupervised Tree-to-Sequence NMT

We modify the standard RNN-based neural machine translation architecture by combining a sequential LSTM decoder with an unsupervised tree-LSTM encoder. This encoder induces hierarchical structure on the source sentence without syntactic supervision. We refer to models containing this encoder as *(unsupervised) tree2seq*.

In this section, we present our unsupervised tree2seq model. Section 3.1 describes the subword-level representations, while section 3.2 explains how the Gumbel tree-LSTM is used to add hierarchies in the encoder. We address top-down representations of the phrase nodes in section 3.3 and explain the attention mechanism in section 3.4.

3.1 Word Node Representations

The hierarchical encoder consists of *word nodes* (nodes corresponding to the subwords of the source sentence) and *phrase nodes* (internal nodes resulting from the induced hierarchies). In order to obtain representations of the word nodes, we run a single-layer bidirectional LSTM over the source sentence; we refer to this LSTM as the *leaf LSTM*.

3.2 Phrase Node Representation

Our proposed unsupervised tree-LSTM encoder uses a Gumbel tree-LSTM (Choi et al., 2018) to obtain the phrase nodes of the source sentence. This encoder introduces unsupervised, discrete hierarchies without modifying the maximum likelihood objective used to train NMT by leveraging straight-through Gumbel softmax (Jang et al., 2017) to sample parsing decisions.

In a Gumbel tree-LSTM, the hidden state $\mathbf{h}_p$ and memory cell $\mathbf{c}_p$ for a given node are computed recursively based on the hidden states and memory nodes of its left and right children ($\mathbf{h}_l$, $\mathbf{h}_r$, $\mathbf{c}_l$, and $\mathbf{c}_r$). This is done as in a standard binary tree-LSTM as follows:

$$\begin{bmatrix} \mathbf{i} \\ \mathbf{f}_l \\ \mathbf{f}_r \\ \mathbf{o} \\ \mathbf{g} \end{bmatrix} = \begin{bmatrix} \sigma \\ \sigma \\ \sigma \\ \sigma \\ \tanh \end{bmatrix} \left(\mathbf{W} \begin{bmatrix} \mathbf{h}_l \\ \mathbf{h}_r \end{bmatrix} + \mathbf{b} \right) \tag{1}$$

$$\mathbf{c}_p = \mathbf{f}_l \odot \mathbf{c}_l + \mathbf{f}_r \odot \mathbf{c}_r + \mathbf{i} \odot \mathbf{g} \tag{2}$$

$$\mathbf{h}_p = \mathbf{o} \odot \tanh(\mathbf{c}_p) \tag{3}$$

where $\mathbf{W}$ is the weight matrix, $\mathbf{b}$ is the bias vector, σ is the sigmoid activation function, and $\odot$ is the element-wise product.

However, the Gumbel tree-LSTM differs from standard tree-LSTMs in that the selection of nodes to merge at each timestep is done in an unsupervised manner. At each timestep, each pair of adjacent nodes is considered for merging, and the hidden states $\widehat{\mathbf{h}}_i$ for each candidate parent representation are computed using equation 3. A composition query vector $\mathbf{q}$, which is simply a vector of trainable weights, is used to obtain a score v_i for each candidate representation as follows:

$$v_i = \frac{\exp\left(\mathbf{q} \cdot \widehat{\mathbf{h}}_i\right)}{\sum_j \exp\left(\mathbf{q} \cdot \widehat{\mathbf{h}}_j\right)} \tag{4}$$

Finally, the straight-through Gumbel softmax estimator (Jang et al., 2017) is used to sample a parent from the candidates $\widehat{\mathbf{h}}_i$ based on these scores v_i; this allows us to sample a hard parent selection while still maintaining differentiability.

This process continues until there is only one remaining node that summarizes the entire sentence; we refer to this as the *root node*. At inference time, straight-through Gumbel softmax is not used; instead, we greedily select the highest-scoring candidate. See Choi et al. (2018) for a more detailed description of Gumbel tree-LSTMs.

Thus, this encoder induces a binary hierarchy over the source sentence. For a sentence of length n, there are n word nodes and $n-1$ phrase nodes (including the root node). We initialize the decoder using the root node; attention to word and/or phrase nodes is described in section 3.4.

3.3 Top-Down Encoder Pass

In the bottom-up tree-LSTM encoder described in the previous section, each node is able to incorporate local information from its respective children; however, no global information is used. Thus, we introduce a top-down pass, which allows the nodes to take global information about the tree into account. We refer to models containing this top-down pass as *top-down tree2seq* models. Note that such a top-down pass has been shown to aid in tree-based NMT with supervised syntactic information (Chen et al., 2017a; Yang et al., 2017); here, we add it to our unsupervised hierarchies.

Our top-down tree implementation is similar to the bidirectional tree-GRU of Kokkinos and Potamianos (2017). The top-down root node $\mathbf{h}^{\downarrow}_{root}$ is defined as follows:

$$\mathbf{h}^{\downarrow}_{root} = \mathbf{h}^{\uparrow}_{root} \tag{5}$$

where $\mathbf{h}^{\uparrow}_{root}$ is the hidden state of the bottom-up root node (calculated using the Gumbel tree-LSTM described in section 3.2).

For each remaining node, including word nodes, the top-down representation $\mathbf{h}^{\downarrow}_{i}$ is computed from its bottom-up hidden state representation $\mathbf{h}^{\uparrow}_{i}$ (calculated using the Gumbel tree-LSTM) and the top-down representation of its parent $\mathbf{h}^{\downarrow}_{p}$ (calculated during the previous top-down steps) using a GRU:

$$\begin{bmatrix} \mathbf{z}^{\downarrow}_{i} \\ \mathbf{r}^{\downarrow}_{i} \end{bmatrix} = \sigma\left(\mathbf{W}^{td}\mathbf{h}^{\uparrow}_{i} + \mathbf{U}^{td}\mathbf{h}^{\downarrow}_{p} + \mathbf{b}^{td}\right) \tag{6}$$

$$\widetilde{\mathbf{h}}^{\downarrow}_{i} = \tanh\left(\mathbf{W}^{td}_{h}\mathbf{h}^{\uparrow}_{i} + \mathbf{U}^{td}_{h}\left(\mathbf{r}^{\downarrow}_{i} \odot \mathbf{h}^{\downarrow}_{p}\right) + \mathbf{b}^{td}_{h}\right) \tag{7}$$

$$\mathbf{h}^{\downarrow}_{i} = \left(1 - \mathbf{z}^{\downarrow}_{i}\right)\mathbf{h}^{\downarrow}_{p} + \mathbf{z}^{\downarrow}_{i}\widetilde{\mathbf{h}}^{\downarrow}_{i} \tag{8}$$

where $\mathbf{W}^{td}$, $\mathbf{U}^{td}$, $\mathbf{W}^{td}_{h}$, and $\mathbf{U}^{td}_{h}$ are weight matrices; $\mathbf{b}^{td}$ and $\mathbf{b}^{td}_{h}$ are bias vectors; and σ is the sigmoid activation function. Note that we do not use different weights for left and right children of a given parent.

Each node needs a final representation to supply to the attention mechanism. Here, the top-down version of each node is used, because the top-down version captures both local and global information about the node.

The decoder is initialized with the top-down representation of the root node. Note, however, that this is identical to the bottom-up representation of the root node, so no additional top-down information is used to initialize the decoder. Since the root node contains information about the entire sentence, this allows the decoder to be initialized with a summary of the source sentence, mirroring standard sequential NMT.

3.4 Attention to Words and Phrases

The standard and top-down tree2seq models take different approaches to attention. The standard (bottom-up) model attends to the intermediate phrase nodes of the tree-LSTM, in addition to the word nodes output by the leaf LSTM. This follows what was done by Eriguchi et al. (2016). We use one attention mechanism for all nodes (word and phrase), making no distinction between different node types. Note that without the attention to the phrase nodes, the bottom-up tree2seq model would be almost equivalent to standard seq2seq, since the word nodes are created using a sequential LSTM (the only difference would be the use of the root node to initialize the decoder).

When the top-down pass (section 3.3) is added to the encoder, the final word nodes contain hierarchical information from the entire tree, as well as sequential information. Therefore, in the top-down tree2seq model, we attend to the top-down word nodes only, ignoring the phrase nodes. We argue that attention to the phrase nodes is unnecessary, since the word nodes summarize the phrase-level information; indeed, in preliminary experiments, attending to phrase nodes did not yield improvements.

4 Experimental Setup

4.1 Data

The models are tested on Tagalog (TL) $\leftrightarrow$ English (EN), Turkish (TR) $\leftrightarrow$ EN, and Romanian (RO) $\leftrightarrow$ EN. These pairs were selected because they range from very low-resource to medium-resource, so we can evaluate the models at various settings. Table 1 displays the number of parallel training sentences for each language pair.

Language Pair	Sentences
TL↔EN	50 962
TR↔EN	207 373
RO↔EN	608 320

Table 1: Amount of parallel sentences for each language pair after preprocessing.

The TR↔EN and RO↔EN data is from the WMT17 and WMT16 shared tasks, respectively (Bojar et al., 2017, 2016). Development is done on newsdev2016 and evaluation on newstest2016. The TL↔EN data is from IARPA MATERIAL Program language collection release IARPA_MATERIAL_BASE-1B-BUILD_v1.0. No monolingual data is used for training.

The data is tokenized and truecased with the Moses scripts (Koehn et al., 2007). We use byte pair encoding (BPE) with 45k merge operations to split words into subwords (Sennrich et al., 2016). Notably, this means that the unsupervised tree encoder induces a binary parse tree over subwords (rather than at the word level).

4.2 Baselines

We compare our models to an RNN-based attentional NMT model; we refer to this model as *seq2seq*. Apart from the encoder, this baseline is identical to our proposed models. We train the seq2seq baseline on unparsed parallel data.

For translations out of English, we also consider an upper bound that uses syntactic supervision; we dub this model *parse2seq*. This is based on the mixed RNN model proposed by Li et al. (2017). We parse the source sentences using the Stanford CoreNLP parser (Manning et al., 2014) and linearize the resulting parses. We parse before applying BPE, and do not add any additional structure to segmented words; thus, final parses are not necessarily binary. This is fed directly into a seq2seq model (with increased maximum source sentence length to account for the parsing tags).

4.3 Implementation

All models are implemented in OpenNMT-py (Klein et al., 2017). They use word embedding size 500, hidden layer size 1000, batch size 64, two layers in the encoder and decoder, and dropout rate 0.3 (Gal and Ghahramani, 2016). We set maximum sentence length to 50 (150 for parse2seq source). Models are trained using Adam (Kingma and Ba, 2015) with learning rate 0.001. For tree-based models, we use a Gumbel temperature of

BLEU	TL→EN	TR→EN	RO→EN
seq2seq	17.9	11.1	**29.3**
tree2seq	**26.1**	12.8	28.6
top-down tree2seq	25.3	**13.2**	28.6

Table 2: BLEU for the baseline and the unsupervised tree2seq systems on *→EN translation.

BLEU	EN→TL	EN→TR	EN→RO
seq2seq	15.9	8.5	27.3
parse2seq	17.1	9.0	**28.4**
tree2seq	**23.1**	9.7	27.3
top-down tree2seq	22.5	**9.8**	27.0

Table 3: BLEU for the baselines and the unsupervised tree2seq systems on EN→* translation.

0.5, which performed best in preliminary experiments. The tree-LSTM component of the unsupervised tree2seq encoders has only a single layer.

We train until convergence on the validation set, and the model with the highest BLEU on the validation set is used to translate the test data. During inference, we set beam size to 12 and maximum length to 100.

5 Results

5.1 Translation Performance

Tables 2 and 3 display BLEU scores for our unsupervised tree2seq models translating into and out of English, respectively. For the lower-resource language pairs, TL↔EN and TR↔EN, the tree2seq and top-down models consistently improve over the seq2seq and parse2seq baselines. However, for the medium-resource language pair (RO↔EN), the unsupervised tree models do not improve over seq2seq, unlike the parse2seq baseline. Thus, inducing hierarchies on the source side is most helpful in very low-resource scenarios.

5.2 Unsupervised Parses

Williams et al. (2017) observed that the parses resulting from Gumbel tree-LSTMs for sentence classification did not seem to fit a known formalism. An examination of the parses induced by our NMT models suggests this as well. Furthermore, the different models (tree2seq and top-down tree2seq) do not seem to learn the same parses for the same language pair. We display example parses induced by the trained systems on a sentence from the test data in Table 4.

	Example Parse
EN→TR tree2seq	(((others have) (((dismissed him) as) a)) (j@@ (oke .)))
EN→TR top-down	((((others have) dismissed) (him as)) ((a (j@@ oke)) .))
EN→RO tree2seq	(((others have) dismissed) (him (((as a) joke) .)))
EN→RO top-down	(others (((have ((dismissed him) (as a))) joke) .))

Table 4: Induced parses on an example sentence from the test data.

Language Pair	tree2seq	top-down
EN→TL	22.1%	16.4%
EN→TR	29.3%	21.3%
EN→RO	27.2%	27.2%
TL→EN	12.7%	22.7%
TR→EN	27.7%	22.9%
RO→EN	30.8%	11.4%

Table 5: Recombined subwords in the test data.

5.3 Subword Recombination

The unsupervised parses are trained over subwords; if the induced hierarchies have a linguistic basis, we would expect the model to combine subwords into words as a first step. For each model, we calculate the percentage of subwords that are recombined correctly; the results are in Table 5. Corroborating the observations in the previous section, only a very low percentage of subwords are correctly recombined for each model. This indicates that the parses the model learns are likely not linguistic. In addition, subword recombination does not seem to correlate with translation performance.

6 Related Work

Most work on adding source hierarchical information to neural machine translation has used supervised syntax. Luong et al. (2016) used a multi-task setup with a shared encoder to parse and translate the source language. Eriguchi et al. (2016) introduced a tree-LSTM encoder for NMT that relied on an external parser to parse the training and test data. The tree-LSTM encoder was improved upon by Chen et al. (2017a) and Yang et al. (2017), who added a top-down pass. Other approaches have used convolutional networks to model source syntax. Chen et al. (2017b) enriched source word representations by extracting information from the dependency tree; a convolutional encoder was then applied to the representations. Bastings et al. (2017) fed source dependency trees into a graph convolutional encoder.

Inducing unsupervised or semi-supervised hierarchies in NMT is a relatively recent research area. Gehring et al. (2017a,b) introduced a fully convolutional model for NMT, which improved over strong sequential baselines. Hashimoto and Tsuruoka (2017) added a latent graph parser to the encoder, allowing it to learn dependency-like source parses in an unsupervised manner. However, they found that pre-training the parser with a small amount of human annotations yielded the best results. Finally, Kim et al. (2017) introduced structured attention networks, which extended basic attention by allowing models to attend to latent structures such as subtrees.

7 Conclusions

In this paper, we have introduced a method for incorporating unsupervised structure into the source side of NMT. For low-resource language pairs, this method yielded strong improvements over sequential and parsed baselines. This technique is useful for adding hierarchies to low-resource NMT when a source-language parser is not available. Further analysis indicated that the induced structures are not similar to known linguistic structures.

In the future, we plan on exploring ways of inducing unsupervised hierarchies on the decoder. Additionally, we would like to try adding some supervision to the source trees, for example in the form of pre-training, in order to see whether actual syntactic information improves our models.

Acknowledgements

This research is based upon work supported in part by the Office of the Director of National Intelligence (ODNI), Intelligence Advanced Research Projects Activity (IARPA), via contract # FA8650-17-C-9117. The views and conclusions contained herein are those of the authors and should not be interpreted as necessarily representing the official policies, either expressed or implied, of ODNI, IARPA, or the U.S. Government. The U.S. Government is authorized to reproduce and distribute reprints for governmental purposes notwithstanding any copyright annotation therein.

References

Dzmitry Bahdanau, Kyunghyun Cho, and Yoshua Bengio. 2015. Neural machine translation by jointly learning to align and translate. In *3rd International Conference on Learning Representations*.

Joost Bastings, Ivan Titov, Wilker Aziz, Diego Marcheggiani, and Khalil Sima'an. 2017. Graph convolutional encoders for syntax-aware neural machine translation. In *Proceedings of the 2017 Conference on Empirical Methods in Natural Language Processing*. Association for Computational Linguistics.

Luisa Bentivogli, Arianna Bisazza, Mauro Cettolo, and Marcello Federico. 2016. Neural versus phrase-based machine translation quality: A case study. In *Proceedings of the 2016 Conference on Empirical Methods in Natural Language Processing*, pages 257–267. Association for Computational Linguistics.

Ondřej Bojar, Rajen Chatterjee, Christian Federmann, Yvette Graham, Barry Haddow, Shujian Huang, Matthias Huck, Philipp Koehn, Qun Liu, Varvara Logacheva, Christof Monz, Matteo Negri, Matt Post, Raphael Rubino, Lucia Specia, and Marco Turchi. 2017. Findings of the 2017 Conference on Machine Translation (WMT17). In *Proceedings of the Second Conference on Machine Translation*, pages 169–214. Association for Computational Linguistics.

Ondřej Bojar, Rajen Chatterjee, Christian Federmann, Yvette Graham, Barry Haddow, Matthias Huck, Antonio Jimeno Yepes, Philipp Koehn, Varvara Logacheva, Christof Monz, Matteo Negri, Aurélie Névéol, Mariana Neves, Martin Popel, Matt Post, Raphael Rubino, Carolina Scarton, Lucia Specia, Marco Turchi, Karin Verspoor, and Marcos Zampieri. 2016. Findings of the 2016 Conference on Machine Translation. In *Proceedings of the First Conference on Machine Translation*, pages 131–198. Association for Computational Linguistics.

Huadong Chen, Shujian Huang, David Chiang, and Jiajun Chen. 2017a. Improved neural machine translation with a syntax-aware encoder and decoder. In *Proceedings of the 55th Annual Meeting of the ACL*, pages 1936–1945. Association for Computational Linguistics.

Kehai Chen, Rui Wang, Masao Utiyama, Lemao Liu, Akihiro Tamura, Eiichiro Sumita, and Tiejun Zhao. 2017b. Neural machine translation with source dependency representation. In *Proceedings of the 2017 Conference on Empirical Methods in Natural Language Processing*, pages 2836–2842. Association for Computational Linguistics.

Kyunghyun Cho, Bart Van Merriënboer, Caglar Gulcehre, Dzmitry Bahdanau, Fethi Bougares, Holger Schwenk, and Yoshua Bengio. 2014. Learning phrase representations using RNN encoder-decoder for statistical machine translation. In *Proceedings of the 2014 Conference on Empirical Methods in Natural Language Processing*, pages 1724–1734. Association for Computational Linguistics.

Jihun Choi, Kang Min Yoo, and Sang-goo Lee. 2018. Learning to compose task-specific tree structures. In *Thirty-Second AAAI Conference on Artificial Intelligence*.

Akiko Eriguchi, Kazuma Hashimoto, and Yoshimasa Tsuruoka. 2016. Tree-to-sequence attentional neural machine translation. In *Proceedings of the 54th Annual Meeting of the ACL*, pages 823–833. Association for Computational Linguistics.

Yarin Gal and Zoubin Ghahramani. 2016. A theoretically grounded application of dropout in recurrent neural networks. In *Advances in Neural Information Processing Systems 29*, pages 1019–1027.

Jonas Gehring, Michael Auli, David Grangier, and Yann N Dauphin. 2017a. A convolutional encoder model for neural machine translation. In *Proceedings of the 55th Annual Meeting of the ACL*, pages 123–135. Association for Computational Linguistics.

Jonas Gehring, Michael Auli, David Grangier, Denis Yarats, and Yann N Dauphin. 2017b. Convolutional sequence to sequence learning. In *Proceedings of the 34th International Conference on Machine Learning*, pages 1243–1252.

Kazuma Hashimoto and Yoshimasa Tsuruoka. 2017. Neural machine translation with source-side latent graph parsing. In *Proceedings of the 2017 Conference on Empirical Methods in Natural Language Processing*. Association for Computational Linguistics.

Sepp Hochreiter and Jürgen Schmidhuber. 1997. Long short-term memory. *Neural Computation*, 9(8):1735–1780.

Eric Jang, Shixiang Gu, and Ben Poole. 2017. Categorical reparameterization with Gumbel-softmax. In *5th International Conference on Learning Representations*.

Nal Kalchbrenner and Phil Blunsom. 2013. Recurrent continuous translation models. In *Proceedings of the 2013 Conference on Empirical Methods in Natural Language Processing*, pages 1700–1709. Association for Computational Linguistics.

Yoon Kim, Carl Denton, Luong Hoang, and Alexander M Rush. 2017. Structured attention networks. In *5th International Conference on Learning Representations*.

Diederik Kingma and Jimmy Ba. 2015. Adam: A method for stochastic optimization. In *3rd International Conference on Learning Representations*.

Guillaume Klein, Yoon Kim, Yuntian Deng, Jean Senellart, and Alexander M Rush. 2017. OpenNMT: Open-source toolkit for neural machine translation. In *Proceedings of the 55th Annual Meeting of the ACL*. Association for Computational Linguistics.

Philipp Koehn, Hieu Hoang, Alexandra Birch, Chris Callison-Burch, Marcello Federico, Nicola Bertoldi, Brooke Cowan, Wade Shen, Christine Moran, Richard Zens, et al. 2007. Moses: open source toolkit for statistical machine translation. In *Proceedings of the 45th Annual Meeting of the ACL*, pages 177–180. Association for Computational Linguistics.

Philipp Koehn and Rebecca Knowles. 2017. Six challenges for neural machine translation. In *Proceedings of the First Workshop on Neural Machine Translation*, pages 28–39. Association for Computational Linguistics.

Filippos Kokkinos and Alexandros Potamianos. 2017. Structural attention neural networks for improved sentiment analysis. In *Proceedings of the 15th Conference of the European Chapter of the Association for Computational Linguistics*, pages 586–591. Association for Computational Linguistics.

Junhui Li, Deyi Xiong, Zhaopeng Tu, Muhua Zhu, Min Zhang, and Guodong Zhou. 2017. Modeling source syntax for neural machine translation. In *Proceedings of the 55th Annual Meeting of the ACL*. Association for Computational Linguistics.

Tal Linzen, Emmanuel Dupoux, and Yoav Goldberg. 2016. Assessing the ability of LSTMs to learn syntax-sensitive dependencies. *Transactions of the Association for Computational Linguistics*, 4:521–535.

Minh-Thang Luong, Quoc V Le, Ilya Sutskever, Oriol Vinyals, and Lukasz Kaiser. 2016. Multi-task sequence to sequence learning. In *4th International Conference on Learning Representations*.

Christopher Manning, Mihai Surdeanu, John Bauer, Jenny Rose Finkel, Steven Bethard, and David McClosky. 2014. The Stanford CoreNLP natural language processing toolkit. In *Proceedings of the 52nd Annual Meeting of the ACL*, pages 55–60. Association for Computational Linguistics.

Rico Sennrich, Barry Haddow, and Alexandra Birch. 2016. Neural machine translation of rare words with subword units. In *Proceedings of the 54th Annual Meeting of the ACL*, pages 1715–1725. Association for Computational Linguistics.

Xing Shi, Inkit Padhi, and Kevin Knight. 2016. Does string-based neural MT learn source syntax? In *Proceedings of the 2016 Conference on Empirical Methods in Natural Language Processing*, pages 1526–1534. Association for Computational Linguistics.

Ilya Sutskever, Oriol Vinyals, and Quoc V Le. 2014. Sequence to sequence learning with neural networks. In *Advances in Neural Information Processing Systems 27*, pages 3104–3112.

Kai Sheng Tai, Richard Socher, and Christopher Manning. 2015. Improved semantic representations from tree-structured long short-term memory networks. In *Proceedings of the 53rd Annual Meeting of the ACL and the 7th International Joint Conference on Natural Language Processing*, pages 1556–1566. Association for Computational Linguistics.

Antonio Toral and Víctor M Sánchez-Cartagena. 2017. A multifaceted evaluation of neural versus phrase-based machine translation for 9 language directions. In *Proceedings of the 15th Conference of the European Chapter of the Association for Computational Linguistics*, pages 1063–1073. Association for Computational Linguistics.

Adina Williams, Andrew Drozdov, and Samuel R Bowman. 2017. Learning to parse from a semantic objective: It works. Is it syntax? *arXiv preprint arXiv:1709.01121*.

Baosong Yang, Derek F Wong, Tong Xiao, Lidia S Chao, and Jingbo Zhu. 2017. Towards bidirectional hierarchical representations for attention-based neural machine translation. In *Proceedings of the 2017 Conference on Empirical Methods in Natural Language Processing*, pages 1432–1441. Association for Computational Linguistics.

Dani Yogatama, Phil Blunsom, Chris Dyer, Edward Grefenstette, and Wang Ling. 2017. Learning to compose words into sentences with reinforcement learning. In *5th International Conference on Learning Representations*.

Latent Tree Learning with Differentiable Parsers: Shift-Reduce Parsing and Chart Parsing

Jean Maillard, Stephen Clark
Computer Laboratory, University of Cambridge
jean@maillard.it, sc609@cam.ac.uk

Abstract

Latent tree learning models represent sentences by composing their words according to an induced parse tree, all based on a downstream task. These models often outperform baselines which use (externally provided) syntax trees to drive the composition order. This work contributes (a) a new latent tree learning model based on shift-reduce parsing, with competitive downstream performance and non-trivial induced trees, and (b) an analysis of the trees learned by our shift-reduce model and by a chart-based model.

1 Introduction

Popular recurrent neural networks in NLP, such as the Gated Recurrent Unit (Cho et al., 2014) and Long Short-Term Memory (Hochreiter and Schmidhuber, 1997), compute sentence representations by reading their words in a sequence. In contrast, the Tree-LSTM architecture (Tai et al., 2015) processes words according to an input parse tree, and manages to achieve improved performance on a number of linguistic tasks.

Recently, Yogatama et al. (2016), Maillard et al. (2017), and Choi et al. (2017) all proposed sentence embedding models which work similarly to a Tree-LSTM, but do not require any parse trees as input. These models function without the assistance of an external automatic parser, and without ever being given any syntactic information as supervision. Rather, they induce parse trees by training on a downstream task such as natural language inference. At the heart of these models is a mechanism to assign trees to sentences – effectively, a natural language parser. Williams et al. (2017a) have recently investigated the tree structures induced by two of these models, trained for a natural language inference task. Their analysis showed that Yogatama et al. (2016) learns mostly trivial left-branching trees, and has inconsistent performance; while Choi et al. (2017) outperforms all baselines (including those using trees from conventional parsers), but learns trees that do not correspond to those of conventional treebanks.

In this paper, we propose a new latent tree learning model. Similarly to Yogatama et al. (2016), we base our approach on shift-reduce parsing. Unlike their work, our model is trained via standard back-propagation, which is made possible by exploiting beam search to obtain an approximate gradient. We show that this model performs well compared to baselines, and induces trees that are not as trivial as those learned by the Yogatama et al. model in the experiments of Williams et al. (2017a).

This paper also presents an analysis of the trees learned by our model, in the style of Williams et al. (2017a). We further analyse the trees learned by the model of Maillard et al. (2017), which had not yet been done, and perform evaluations on both the SNLI data (Bowman et al., 2015) and the MultiNLI data (Williams et al., 2017b). The former corpus had not been used for the evaluation of trees of Williams et al. (2017a), and we find that it leads to more consistent induced trees.

2 Related work

The first neural model which learns to both parse a sentence and embed it for a downstream task is by Socher et al. (2011). The authors train the model's parsing component on an auxiliary task, based on recursive autoencoders, while the rest of the model is trained for sentiment analysis.

Bowman et al. (2016) propose the "Shift-reduce Parser-Interpreter Neural Network", a model which obtains syntax trees using an integrated shift-reduce parser (trained on gold-

Proceedings of the Workshop on the Relevance of Linguistic Structure in Neural Architectures for NLP, pages 13–18
Melbourne, Australia, July 19, 2018.

standard trees), and uses the resulting structure to drive composition with Tree-LSTMs.

Yogatama et al. (2016) is the first model to jointly train its parsing and sentence embedding components. They base their model on shift-reduce parsing. Their parser is not differentiable, so they rely on reinforcement learning for training.

Maillard et al. (2017) propose an alternative approach, inspired by CKY parsing. The algorithm is made differentiable by using a soft-gating approach, which approximates discrete candidate selection by a probabilistic mixture of the constituents available in a given cell of the chart. This makes it possible to train with backpropagation.

Choi et al. (2017) use an approach similar to easy-first parsing. The parsing decisions are discrete, but the authors use the Straight-Through Gumbel-Softmax estimator (Jang et al., 2017) to obtain an approximate gradient and are thus able to train with backpropagation.

Williams et al. (2017a) investigate the trees produced by Yogatama et al. (2016) and Choi et al. (2017) when trained on two natural language inference corpora, and analyse the results. They find that the former model induces almost entirely left-branching trees, while the latter performs well but has inconsistent trees across re-runs with different parameter initializations.

A number of other neural models have also been proposed which create a tree encoding during parsing, but unlike the above architectures rely on traditional parse trees. Le and Zuidema (2015) propose a sentence embedding model based on CKY, taking as input a parse forest from an automatic parser. Dyer et al. (2016) propose RNNG, a probabilistic model of phrase-structure trees and sentences, with an integrated parser that is trained on gold standard trees.

3 Models

CKY The model of Maillard et al. (2017) is based on chart parsing, and effectively works like a CKY parser (Cocke, 1969; Kasami, 1965; Younger, 1967) using a grammar with a single non-terminal A with rules $A \rightarrow A\ A$ and $A \rightarrow \alpha$, where α is any terminal. The parse chart is built bottom-up incrementally, like in a standard CKY parser. When ambiguity arises, due to the multiple ways to form a constituent, all options are computed using a Tree-LSTM, and scored. The constituent is then represented as a weighted sum of all possible options, using the normalised scores as weights. In order for this weighted sum to approximate a discrete selection, a temperature hyperparameter is used in the softmax. This process is repeated for the whole chart, and the sentence representation is given by the topmost cell.

We noticed in our experiments that the weighted sum still occasionally assigned non-trivial weight to more than one option. The model was thus able to utilize multiple inferred trees, rather than a single one, which would have potentially given it an advantage over other latent tree models. Hence for fairness, in our experiments we replace the softmax-with-temperature of Maillard et al. (2017) with a softmax followed by a straight-through estimator (Bengio et al., 2013). In the forward pass, this approach is equivalent to an argmax function; while in the backward pass it is equivalent to a softmax. Effectively, this means that a single tree is selected during forward evaluation, but the training signal can still propagate to every path during backpropagation. This change did not noticeably affect performance on development data.

Beam Search Shift-Reduce We propose a model based on beam search shift-reduce parsing (BSSR). The parser works with a queue, which holds the embeddings for the nodes representing individual words which are still to be processed; and a stack, which holds the embeddings of the nodes which have already been computed. A standard binary Tree-LSTM function (Tai et al., 2015) is used to compute the d-dimensional embeddings of nodes:

$$
\begin{aligned}
\begin{bmatrix} \boldsymbol{i} \\ \boldsymbol{f}_L \\ \boldsymbol{f}_R \\ \boldsymbol{u} \\ \boldsymbol{o} \end{bmatrix} &= \mathbf{W}\boldsymbol{w} + \mathbf{U}\boldsymbol{h}_L + \mathbf{V}\boldsymbol{h}_R + \boldsymbol{b}, \\
\boldsymbol{c} &= \boldsymbol{c}_L \odot \sigma(\boldsymbol{f}_L) + \boldsymbol{c}_R \odot \sigma(\boldsymbol{f}_R) \\
&\quad + \tanh(\boldsymbol{u}) \odot \sigma(\boldsymbol{i}), \\
\boldsymbol{h} &= \sigma(\boldsymbol{o}) \odot \tanh(\boldsymbol{c}),
\end{aligned}
$$

where $\mathbf{W}, \mathbf{U}$ are learned $5d \times d$ matrices, and $\boldsymbol{b}$ is a learned $5d$ vector. The d-dimensional vectors $\sigma(\boldsymbol{i}), \sigma(\boldsymbol{f}_L), \sigma(\boldsymbol{f}_R)$ are known as *input* gate and *left-* and *right-forget* gates, respectively. $\sigma(\boldsymbol{o}_t)$ and $\tanh(\boldsymbol{u}_t)$ are known as *output* gate and *candidate update*. The vector $\boldsymbol{w}$ is a word embedding, while $\boldsymbol{h}_L, \boldsymbol{h}_R$ and $\boldsymbol{c}_L, \boldsymbol{c}_R$ are the childrens' $\boldsymbol{h}$- and $\boldsymbol{c}$-states. At the beginning, the queue contains embeddings for the nodes corresponding to single words. These are obtained by computing the Tree-LSTM with w set to the word embedding, and $h_{L/R}, c_{L/R}$ set to zero. When a SHIFT action is performed, the topmost element of the queue is popped, and pushed onto the stack. When a REDUCE action is performed, the top two elements of the stack are popped. A new node is then computed as their parent, by passing the children through the Tree-LSTM, with $w = 0$. The new node is then pushed onto the stack.

Parsing actions are scored with a simple multilayer perceptron, which looks at the top two stack elements and the top queue element:

$$r = \mathbf{W}_{s1} \cdot h_{s1} + \mathbf{W}_{s2} \cdot h_{s2} + \mathbf{W}_q \cdot h_{q1},$$
$$p = \mathrm{softmax}\,(a + \mathbf{A} \cdot \tanh r),$$

where h_{s1}, h_{s2}, h_{q1} are the h-states of the top two elements of the stack and the top element of the queue, respectively. The three $\mathbf{W}$ matrices have dimensions $d \times d$ and are learned; a is a learned 2-dimensional vector; and $\mathbf{A}$ is a learned $2 \times d$ vector. The final scores are given by $\log p$, and the best action is greedily selected at every time step. The sentence representation is given by the h-state of the top element of the stack after $2n - 1$ steps.

In order to make this model trainable with gradient descent, we use beam search to select the b best action sequences, where the score of a sequence of actions is given by the sum of the scores of the individual actions. The final sentence representation is then a weighted sum of the sentence representations from the elements of the beam. The weights are given by the respective scores of the action sequences, normalised by a softmax and passed through a straight-through estimator. This is equivalent to having an argmax on the forward pass, which discretely selects the top-scoring beam element, and a softmax in the backward pass.

4 Experimental Setup

Data To match the settings of Maillard et al. (2017), we run experiments with the SNLI corpus (Bowman et al., 2015). We additionally run a second set of experiments with the MultiNLI data (Williams et al., 2017b), and to match Williams et al. (2017a) we augment the MultiNLI training data with the SNLI training data. We call this augmented training set *MultiNLI+*. For the MultiNLI+ experiments, we use the *matched* versions of the development and test sets. We use pre-trained 100D GloVe embeddings[1] (Pennington et al., 2014) for performance reasons, and fine-tune them during training. Unlike Williams et al. (2017a), we do not use a bidirectional leaf transformation. Models are optimised with Adam (Kingma and Ba, 2014), and we train five instances of every model. For BSSR, we use a beam size of 50, and let it linearly decrease to its final size of 5 over the first two epochs.

Model	SNLI	MultiNLI+
Prior work: Baselines		
100D LSTM (Yogatama)	80.2	—
300D LSTM (Williams)	82.6	69.1
100D Tree-LSTM (Yogatama)	78.5	—
300D SPINN (Williams)	82.2	67.5
Prior work: Latent Tree Models		
100D ST-Gumbel (Choi)	81.9	—
300D ST-Gumbel (Williams)	83.3	**69.5**
300D ST-Gumbel† (Williams)	**83.7**	67.5
100D CKY (Maillard)	81.6	—
100D RL-SPINN (Yogatama)	80.5	—
300D RL-SPINN† (Williams)	82.3	67.4
This work: Latent Tree Models		
100D CKY (Ours)	82.2	69.1
100D BSSR (Ours)	83.0	69.0

Table 1: SNLI and MultiNLI (matched) test set accuracy. †: results are for the model variant without the leaf RNN transformation.

Setup To assign the labels of *entails*, *contradicts*, or *neutral* to the pairs of sentences, we follow Yogatama et al. (2016) and concatenate the two sentence embeddings, their element-wise product, and their squared Euclidean distance into a vector v. We then calculate $q = \mathrm{ReLU}\,(\mathbf{C} \cdot v + c)$, where $\mathbf{C}$ is a $200 \times 4d$ learned matrix and c a 200-dimensional learned bias; and finally predict $p(y = c \mid q) \propto \exp(\mathbf{B} \cdot q + b)$ where $\mathbf{B}$ is a 3×200 matrix and b is 3-dimensional.

5 Experiments

For each model and dataset, we train five instances using different random initialisations, for a total of $2 \times 2 \times 5 = 20$ instances.

NLI Accuracy We measure SNLI and MultiNLI test set accuracy for CKY and BSSR. The aim is to ensure that they perform reasonably, and are in line with other latent tree learning models of a similar size and complexity. Results for the best mod-

[1] https://nlp.stanford.edu/projects/glove/

Dataset	Model	Self-F1	F1 w.r.t. Left Branching μ (σ)	max	Right Branching μ (σ)	max	Stanford Parser μ (σ)	max
MultiNLI+	300D SPINN (Williams)	71.5	19.3 (0.4)	19.8	36.9 (3.4)	**42.6**	**70.2** (3.6)	**74.5**
MultiNLI+	300D ST-Gumbel (Williams)	49.9	32.6 (2.0)	35.6	**37.5** (2.4)	40.3	23.7 (0.9)	25.2
MultiNLI+	300D ST-Gumbel† (Williams)	41.2	30.8 (1.2)	32.3	35.6 (3.3)	39.9	27.5 (1.0)	29.0
MultiNLI+	300D RL-SPINN† (Williams)	**98.5**	**99.1** (0.6)	**99.8**	10.7 (0.2)	11.1	18.1 (0.1)	18.2
MultiNLI+	100D CKY (Ours)	45.9	32.9 (1.9)	35.1	31.5 (2.3)	35.1	23.7 (1.1)	25.0
MultiNLI+	100D BSSR (Ours)	46.6	40.6 (6.5)	47.6	24.2 (6.0)	27.7	23.5 (1.8)	26.2
MultiNLI+	*Random Trees* (Williams)	32.6	27.9 (0.1)	27.9	28.0 (0.1)	28.1	27.0 (0.1)	27.1
SNLI	100D RL-SPINN (Yogatama)	—	—	41.4	—	19.9	—	**41.7**
SNLI	100D CKY (Ours)	59.2	43.9 (2.2)	46.9	**33.7** (2.6)	**36.7**	30.3 (1.1)	32.1
SNLI	100D BSSR (Ours)	**60.0**	**48.8** (5.2)	**53.9**	26.5 (6.9)	34.0	**32.8** (3.5)	36.4
SNLI	*Random Trees* (Ours)	35.9	32.3 (0.1)	32.4	32.5 (0.1)	32.6	32.3 (0.1)	32.5

Table 2: Unlabelled F1 scores of the trees induced by various models against: other runs of the same model, fully left- and right-branching trees, and Stanford Parser trees provided with the datasets. The baseline results on MultiNLI are from Williams et al. (2017a). †: results are for the model variant without the leaf RNN transformation.

els, chosen based on development set performance, are reported in Table 1.

While our models do not reach the state of the art, they perform at least as well as other latent tree models using 100D embeddings, and are competitive with some 300D models. They also outperform the 100D Tree-LSTM of Yogatama et al. (2016), which is given syntax trees, and match or outperform 300D SPINN, which is explicitly trained to parse.

Self-consistency Next, we examine the consistency of the trees produced for the development sets. Adapting the code of Williams et al. (2017a), we measure the models' *self F1*, defined as the unlabelled F1 between trees by two instances of the same model (given by different random initializations), averaged over all possible pairs. Results are shown in Table 2. In order to test whether BSSR and CKY learn similar grammars, we calculate the *inter-model F1*, defined as the unlabelled F1 between instances of BSSR and CKY trained on the same data, averaged over all possible pairs. We find an average F1 of 42.6 for MultiNLI+ and 55.0 for SNLI, both above the random baseline.

Our Self F1 results are all above the baseline of random trees. For MultiNLI+, they are in line with ST-Gumbel. Remarkably, the models trained on SNLI are noticeably more self-consistent. This shows that the specifics of the training data play an important role, even when the downstream task is the same. A possible explanation is that MultiNLI has longer sentences, as well as multiple genres, including telephone conversations which often do not constitute full sentences (Williams et al., 2017b). This would require the models to learn how to parse a wide variety of styles of data. It is also interesting to note that the inter-model F1 scores are not much lower than the self F1 scores. This shows that, given the same training data, the grammars learned by the two different models are not much more different than the grammars learned by two instances of the same model.

F1 Scores Finally, we investigate whether these models learn grammars that are recognisably left-branching, right-branching, or similar to the trees produced by the Stanford Parser which are included in both datasets. We report the unlabelled F1 between these and the trees from from our models in Table 2, averaged over the five model instances. We show mean, standard deviation, and maximum.

We find a slight preference from BSSR and the SNLI-trained CYK towards left-branching structures. Our models do not learn anything that resembles the trees from the Stanford Parser, and have an F1 score with them which is at or below the random baseline. Our results match those of Williams et al. (2017a), which show that whatever these models learn, it does not resemble PTB grammar.

6 Conclusions

First, we proposed a new latent tree learning model based on a shift-reduce parser. Unlike a previous model based on the same parsing technique, we showed that our approach does not learn trivial trees, and performs competitively on the downstream task.

Second, we analysed the trees induced by our shift-reduce model and a latent tree model based on chart parsing. Our results confirmed those of previous work on different models, showing that the learned grammars do not resemble PTB-style trees (Williams et al., 2017a). Remarkably, we saw that the two different models tend to learn grammars which are not much more different than those learned by two instances of the same model.

Finally, our experiments highlight the importance of the choice of training data used for latent tree learning models, even when the downstream task is the same. Our results suggest that MultiNLI, which has on average longer sentences coming from different genres, might be hindering the current models' ability to learn consistent grammars. For future work investigating this phenomenon, it may be interesting to train models using only the written genres parts of MultiNLI, or MultiNLI without the SNLI corpus.

Acknowledgments

We are grateful to Chris Dyer for the several productive discussions. We would like to thank the anonymous reviewers for their helpful comments.

References

Yoshua Bengio, Nicholas Léonard, and Aaron C. Courville. 2013. Estimating or propagating gradients through stochastic neurons for conditional computation. *CoRR*, abs/1308.3432.

Samuel R. Bowman, Gabor Angeli, Christopher Potts, and Christopher D. Manning. 2015. A large annotated corpus for learning natural language inference. In *Proceedings of the 2015 Conference on Empirical Methods in Natural Language Processing (EMNLP)*.

Samuel R Bowman, Jon Gauthier, Abhinav Rastogi, Raghav Gupta, Christopher D Manning, and Christopher Potts. 2016. A fast unified model for parsing and sentence understanding. In *Proceedings of the 54th Annual Meeting of the Association for Computational Linguistics (Volume 1: Long Papers)*, pages 1466–1477, Berlin, Germany. Association for Computational Linguistics.

Kyunghyun Cho, Bart van Merrienboer, Caglar Gulcehre, Dzmitry Bahdanau, Fethi Bougares, Holger Schwenk, and Yoshua Bengio. 2014. Learning phrase representations using rnn encoder–decoder for statistical machine translation. In *Proceedings of the 2014 Conference on Empirical Methods in Natural Language Processing (EMNLP)*, pages 1724–1734, Doha, Qatar. Association for Computational Linguistics.

Jihun Choi, Kang Min Yoo, and Sang-goo Lee. 2017. Learning to compose task-specific tree structures. *arXiv*, abs/1707.02786.

John Cocke. 1969. *Programming Languages and Their Compilers: Preliminary Notes*. Courant Institute of Mathematical Sciences, New York University.

Chris Dyer, Adhiguna Kuncoro, Miguel Ballesteros, and Noah A. Smith. 2016. Recurrent neural network grammars. In *Proceedings of the 2016 Conference of the North American Chapter of the Association for Computational Linguistics: Human Language Technologies*, pages 199–209, San Diego, California. Association for Computational Linguistics.

Sepp Hochreiter and Jürgen Schmidhuber. 1997. Long short-term memory. *Neural Comput.*, 9(8):1735–1780.

Eric Jang, Shixiang Gu, and Ben Poole. 2017. Categorical reparameterization with gumbel-softmax.

T. Kasami. 1965. An efficient recognition and syntax analysis algorithm for context-free languages. Technical Report AFCRL-65-758, Air Force Cambridge Research Laboratory, Bedford, MA.

Diederik P. Kingma and Jimmy Ba. 2014. Adam: A method for stochastic optimization. *arXiv*, abs/1412.6980.

Phong Le and Willem Zuidema. 2015. The forest convolutional network: Compositional distributional semantics with a neural chart and without binarization. In *Proceedings of the 2015 Conference on Empirical Methods in Natural Language Processing*, pages 1155–1164, Lisbon, Portugal. Association for Computational Linguistics.

Jean Maillard, Stephen Clark, and Dani Yogatama. 2017. Jointly learning sentence embeddings and syntax with unsupervised tree-lstms. *arXiv*, abs/1705.09189.

Jeffrey Pennington, Richard Socher, and Christopher D. Manning. 2014. Glove: Global vectors for word representation. In *Empirical Methods in Natural Language Processing (EMNLP)*, pages 1532–1543.

Richard Socher, Jeffrey Pennington, Eric H. Huang, Andrew Y. Ng, and Christopher D. Manning. 2011. Semi-supervised recursive autoencoders for predicting sentiment distributions. In *Proceedings of the 2011 Conference on Empirical Methods in Natural Language Processing*, pages 151–161, Edinburgh, Scotland, UK. Association for Computational Linguistics.

Kai Sheng Tai, Richard Socher, and Christopher D. Manning. 2015. Improved semantic representations from tree-structured long short-term memory networks. In *Proceedings of the 53rd Annual Meeting of the Association for Computational Linguistics and the 7th International Joint Conference on Natural Language Processing (Volume 1: Long Papers)*, pages 1556–1566, Beijing, China. Association for Computational Linguistics.

Adina Williams, Andrew Drozdov, and Samuel R. Bowman. 2017a. Learning to parse from a semantic objective: It works. is it syntax?

Adina Williams, Nikita Nangia, and Samuel R. Bowman. 2017b. A broad-coverage challenge corpus for sentence understanding through inference. *arXiv*, abs/1704.05426.

Dani Yogatama, Phil Blunsom, Chris Dyer, Edward Grefenstette, and Wang Ling. 2016. Learning to compose words into sentences with reinforcement learning. *arXiv*, abs/1611.09100.

Daniel H. Younger. 1967. Recognition and parsing of context-free languages in time n^3. *Information and Control*, 10:189–208.

Syntax Helps ELMo Understand Semantics: Is Syntax Still Relevant in a Deep Neural Architecture for SRL?

Emma Strubell **Andrew McCallum**
College of Information and Computer Sciences
University of Massachusetts Amherst
{strubell, mccallum}@cs.umass.edu

Abstract

Do unsupervised methods for learning rich, contextualized token representations obviate the need for explicit modeling of linguistic structure in neural network models for semantic role labeling (SRL)? We address this question by incorporating the massively successful ELMo embeddings (Peters et al., 2018) into LISA (Strubell and McCallum, 2018), a strong, linguistically-informed neural network architecture for SRL. In experiments on the CoNLL-2005 shared task we find that though ELMo out-performs typical word embeddings, beginning to close the gap in F1 between LISA with predicted and gold syntactic parses, syntactically-informed models still out-perform syntax-free models when both use ELMo, especially on out-of-domain data. Our results suggest that linguistic structures are indeed still relevant in this golden age of deep learning for NLP.

1 Introduction

Many state-of-the-art NLP models are now "end-to-end" deep neural network architectures which eschew explicit linguistic structures as input in favor of operating directly on raw text (Ma and Hovy, 2016; Lee et al., 2017; Tan et al., 2018). Recently, Peters et al. (2018) proposed a method for unsupervised learning of rich, contextually-encoded token representations which, when supplied as input word representations in end-to-end models, further increased these models' performance by up to 25% across many NLP tasks. The immense success of these linguistically-agnostic models brings into question whether linguistic structures such as syntactic parse trees still provide any additional benefits in a deep neural network architecture for e.g. semantic role labeling (SRL).

In this work, we aim to begin to answer this question by experimenting with incorporating the ELMo embeddings of Peters et al. (2018) into LISA (Strubell and McCallum, 2018), a "linguistically-informed" deep neural network architecture for SRL which, when given weaker GloVe embeddings as inputs (Pennington et al., 2014), has been shown to leverage syntax to out-perform a state-of-the-art, linguistically-agnostic end-to-end SRL model.

In experiments on the CoNLL-2005 English SRL shared task, we find that, while the ELMo representations out-perform GloVe and begin to close the performance gap between LISA with predicted and gold syntactic parses, syntactically-informed models still out-perform syntax-free models, especially on out-of-domain data. Our results suggest that with the right modeling, incorporating linguistic structures can indeed further improve strong neural network models for NLP.

2 Models

We are interested in assessing whether linguistic information is still beneficial in addition to deep, contextualized ELMo word embeddings in a neural network model for SRL. Towards this end, our base model for experimentation is Linguistically-Informed Self-Attention (LISA) (Strubell and McCallum, 2018), a deep neural network model which uses multi-head self-attention in the style of Vaswani et al. (2017) for multi-task learning (Caruana, 1993) across SRL, predicate detection, part-of-speech tagging and syntactic parsing. Syntax is incorporated by training one self-attention head to attend to each token's syntactic head, allowing it to act as an oracle providing syntactic in-

Proceedings of the Workshop on the Relevance of Linguistic Structure in Neural Architectures for NLP, pages 19–27
Melbourne, Australia, July 19, 2018.

formation to further layers used to predict semantic roles. We summarize the key points of LISA in §2.1.

Strubell and McCallum (2018) showed that LISA out-performs syntax-free models when both use GloVe word embeddings as input, which, due to their availability, size and large training corpora, are typically used as input to end-to-end NLP models. In this work, we replace those token representations with ELMo representations to assess whether ELMo embeddings are sufficiently rich to obviate the need for explicit representations of syntax, or the model still benefits from syntactic information in addition to the rich ELMo encodings. In §2.2 and §2.3 we summarize how GloVe and ELMo embeddings, respectively, are incorporated into this model.

2.1 LISA SRL model

2.1.1 Neural network token encoder

The input to LISA is a sequence $\mathcal{X}$ of T token representations x_t. The exact form of these representations when using GloVe embeddings is described in §2.2, and for ELMo described in §2.3. Following Vaswani et al. (2017), we add a sinusoidal positional encoding to these vectors since the self-attention has no inherent mechanism for modeling token position.

These token representations are supplied to a series of J multi-head self-attention layers similar to those that make up the encoder model of Vaswani et al. (2017). We denote the jth layer with the function $S^{(j)}(\cdot)$ and the output of that layer for token t as $s_t^{(j)}$:

$$s_t^{(j)} = S^{(j)}(s_t^{(j-1)}) \tag{1}$$

Each $S^{(j)}(\cdot)$ consists of two components: (a) multi-head self-attention and (b) a convolutional layer. For brevity, we will detail (a) here as it is how we incorporate syntax into the model, but we leave the reader to refer to Strubell and McCallum (2018) for more details on (b).

The multi-head self attention consists of H attention heads, each of which learns a distinct attention function to attend to all of the tokens in the sequence. This self-attention is performed for each token for each head, and the results of the H self-attentions are concatenated to form the final self-attended representation for each token.

Specifically, consider the matrix $S^{(j-1)}$ of T token representations at layer $j-1$. For each attention head h, we project this matrix into distinct key, value and query representations $K_h^{(j)}$, $V_h^{(j)}$ and $Q_h^{(j)}$ of dimensions $T \times d_k$, $T \times d_q$, and $T \times d_v$, respectively. We can then multiply $Q_h^{(j)}$ by $K_h^{(j)}$ to obtain a $T \times T$ matrix of attention weights $A_h^{(j)}$ between each pair of tokens in the sentence. Following Vaswani et al. (2017) we perform scaled dot-product attention: We scale the weights by the inverse square root of their embedding dimension and normalize with the softmax function to produce a distinct distribution for each token over all the tokens in the sentence:

$$A_h^{(j)} = \mathrm{softmax}(d_k^{-0.5} Q_h^{(j)} K_h^{(j)^T}) \tag{2}$$

These attention weights are then multiplied by $V_h^{(j)}$ for each token to obtain the self-attended token representations $M_h^{(j)}$:

$$M_h^{(j)} = A_h^{(j)} V_h^{(j)} \tag{3}$$

Row t of $M_h^{(j)}$, the self-attended representation for token t at layer j, is thus the weighted sum with respect to t (given by $A_h^{(j)}$) over the token representations in $V_h^{(j)}$. The representations for each attention head are concatenated, and this representation is fed through a convolutional layer to produce $s_t^{(j)}$. In all of our models, we use $J = 4$, $H = 8$ and $d_k = d_q = d_v = 64$.

2.1.2 Incorporating syntax

LISA incorporates syntax by training one attention head to attend to each token's parent in a syntactic dependency parse tree. At layer j_p, $H - 1$ heads are left to learn on their own to attend to relevant tokens in the sentence, while one head h_p is trained with an auxiliary objective which encourages the head to put all attention weight on each token's syntactic parent. Denoting the entry of $A_{h_p}^{(j_p)}$ corresponding to the attention from token t to token q as a_{tq}, then we model the probability that q is the head of t as: $P(q = \mathrm{head}(t) \mid \mathcal{X}) = a_{tq}$. Trained in this way, $A_{h_p}^{(j_p)}$ emits a directed graph, where each token's syntactic parent is that which is assigned the highest attention weight. During training, this head's attention weights are set to match the gold parse: $A_{h_p}^{(j_p)}$ is set to the adjacency matrix of the parse tree,[1] allowing downstream layers to learn to use the parse information

[1]Roots are represented by self-loops.

tion throughout training. In our experiments we set $j_p = 3$.

In this way, LISA is trained to use $A_{h_p}^{(j_p)}$ as an oracle providing parse information to downstream layers. This representation is flexible, allowing LISA to use its own predicted parse, or a parse produced by another dependency parser. Since LISA is trained to leverage gold parse information, as higher-accuracy dependency parses become available, they can be provided to LISA to improve SRL without requiring re-training of the SRL model.

2.1.3 Predicting POS and predicates

LISA is also trained to predict parts-of-speech and predicates using hard parameter sharing (Caruana, 1993). At layer j_{pos}, the token representation $s_t^{(j_{pos})}$ is provided as features for a multiclass classifier into the joint label space of part-of-speech and (binary) predicate labels: For each part-of-speech tag which is the tag for a predicate in the training data, we add a tag of the form TAG;PREDICATE. Locally-normalized probabilities are computed using the softmax function, and we minimize the sum of this loss term with the SRL and syntax losses. In our experiments we use $j_{pos} = 2$.

2.1.4 Predicting semantic roles

LISA's final network representations $S^{(J)}$ are used to predict semantic roles. Each token's final representation $s_t^{(J)}$ is projected to distinct *predicate* and *role* representations s_t^{pred} and s_t^{role}. Each predicted predicate[2] is scored against all other tokens' role representations to produce per-label scores for each predicate-token pair using a bilinear operator U. Per-label scores across semantic roles with respect to predicate f and token t are thus given by:

$$s_{ft} = s_f^{pred} U s_t^{role} \tag{4}$$

With the locally-normalized probability of the correct role label y_{ft} given by: $P(y_{ft} \mid \mathcal{X}) \propto \text{softmax}(s_{ft})$. At test time, we use Viterbi decoding to enforce BIO constraints with fixed transition probabilities between tags obtained from the training data.

[2]During training, semantic role predictions are conditioned on the gold predicates. At test time they are conditioned on LISA's predicted predicates (§2.1.3).

2.2 GLoVe embedding model

The GloVe word embedding model (Pennington et al., 2014), like word2vec's skip-gram and CBOW (Mikolov et al., 2013) algorithms, is a shallow, log-bilinear embedding model for learning unsupervised representations of words based on the intuition that words which occur in similar contexts should have similar representations. GloVe Vectors are learned for each word in a fixed vocabulary by regressing on entries in the word co-occurrence matrix constructed from a large corpus: The dot product between two words' embeddings should equal the log probability of the words' co-occurrence in the data. We refer the reader to Pennington et al. (2014) for a more detailed description of the model.

We incorporate pre-trained GloVe embeddings into our model following Strubell and McCallum (2018): We fix the pre-trained embeddings and add a learned word embedding representation to the pre-trained word vectors, following the intuition that fixing the pre-trained embeddings and learning a residual word representation keeps words observed during training from drifting too far away from the pre-trained representations of unobserved words. We then feed these representations through K width-3 convolutional layers with residual connections. See Strubell and McCallum (2018) for more details on these layers. In our experiments we use $K = 2$ and convolutional filters of size 1024. We use the typical 100 dimensional GloVe embeddings pre-trained on 6 billion tokens of text from Wikipedia and Gigaword.[3]

2.3 ELMo embedding model

The ELMo model (Peters et al., 2018) produces deep, contextually embedded token representations by training stacked convolutional, highway and bi-directional LSTM (bi-LSTM) layers on a large corpus of text with an unsupervised language modeling (LM) objective. The expressiveness of this model compared to GloVe-style embeddings models differs in two key ways: (1) ELMo observes the entire sentence of context to model each token rather than relying on a small, fixed window and (2) ELMo does not rely on a fixed vocabulary of token embeddings, instead building up token representations from characters.

The ELMo architecture enhances the bidirec-

[3]`https://nlp.stanford.edu/projects/glove/`

tional LM architecture from Peters et al. (2017). The model first composes character embeddings into word type embeddings using a convolutional layer followed by highway layers. Then these token representations are passed to multiple bi-LSTM layers, all of which are trained end-to-end to jointly optimize forward and backward LM objectives. ELMo additionally learns a small number of task-specific parameters to compose and scale the outputs of each LM, producing a task-specific embedding for each token in context. The intuition behind these task-specific parameters is that different tasks will benefit from different weightings of shallower and deeper LM representations. For example, parsing might favor earlier layers which better capture syntactic patterns, whereas question answering might favor later layers which capture higher level semantics of the sentence. Peters et al. (2018) experiment with adding ELMo embeddings on the input and output of some architectures, with varying results across different tasks. We incorporate ELMo embeddings into the model by keeping the pre-trained parameters fixed but learning a task-specific combination of the layer outputs which we feed as inputs to our model, as described in Peters et al. (2018). We follow their implementation for the SRL architecture of (He et al., 2017) and use the ELMo embeddings only as input to the model. We refer to Peters et al. (2018) for more details on this model.

We use the pre-trained TensorFlow ELMo model[4], which consists of one character-level convolutional layer with 2048 filters followed by two highway layers followed by two bi-LSTM layers with 4096 hidden units. All three layers are projected down to 512 dimensional representations over which our task-specific parameters are learned. This model is trained on the 1B Word Benchmark (Chelba et al., 2014), which consists of filtered English newswire, news commentary and European parliament proceedings from the WMT '11 shared task.

3 Related work

Our experiments are based on the LISA model of Strubell and McCallum (2018), who showed that their method for incorporating syntax into a deep neural network architecture for SRL improves SRL F1 with predicted predicates on CoNLL-2005 and CoNLL-2012 data, including on out-of-domain test data. Other recent works have also found syntax to improve neural SRL models when evaluated on data from the CoNLL-2009 shared task: Roth and Lapata (2016) use LSTMs to embed syntactic dependency paths, and Marcheggiani and Titov (2017) incorporate syntax using graph convolutional neural networks over predicted dependency parse trees. In contrast to this work, Marcheggiani and Titov (2017) found that their syntax-aware model did not out-perform a syntax-agnostic model on out-of-domain data.

The idea that an SRL model should incorporate syntactic structure is not new, since many semantic formalities are defined with respect to syntax. Many of the first approaches to SRL (Pradhan et al., 2005; Surdeanu et al., 2007; Johansson and Nugues, 2008; Toutanova et al., 2008; Punyakanok et al., 2008), spearheaded by the CoNLL-2005 shared task (Carreras and Màrquez, 2005), achieved success by relying on syntax-heavy linguistic features as input for a linear model, combined with structured inference which could also take syntax into account. Täckström et al. (2015) showed that most of these constraints could more efficiently be enforced by exact inference in a dynamic program. While most techniques required a predicted parse as input, Sutton and McCallum (2005) modeled syntactic parsing and SRL with a joint graphical model, and Lewis et al. (2015) jointly modeled SRL and CCG semantic parsing. Collobert et al. (2011) were among the first to use a neural network model for SRL, using a CNN over word embeddings combined with globally-normalized inference. However, their model failed to out-perform non-neural models, both with and without multi-task learning with other NLP tagging tasks such as part-of-speech tagging and chunking. FitzGerald et al. (2015) were among the first to successfully employ neural networks, achieving the state-of-the-art by embedding lexicalized features and providing the embeddings as factors in the model of Täckström et al. (2015).

Recently there has been a move away from SRL models which explicitly incorporate syntactic knowledge through features and structured inference towards models which rely on deep neural networks to learn syntactic structure and long-range dependencies from the data. Zhou and Xu (2015) were the first to achieve state-of-the-art results using 8 layers of bidirectional LSTM combined with inference in a linear-chain conditional

[4] `https://github.com/allenai/bilm-tf`

random field (Lafferty et al., 2001). Marcheggiani et al. (2017) and He et al. (2017) also achieved state-of-the-art results using deep LSTMs with no syntactic features. While most previous work assumes that gold predicates are given, like this work and Strubell and McCallum (2018), He et al. (2017) evaluate on predicted predicates, though they train a separate model for predicate detection. Most recently, Tan et al. (2018) achieved the state-of-the art on the CoNLL-2005 and 2012 shared tasks with gold predicates and no syntax using 10 layers of self-attention, and on CoNLL-2012 with gold predicates Peters et al. (2018) increase the score of He et al. (2017) by more than 3 F1 points by incorporating ELMo embeddings into their model, out-performing ensembles from Tan et al. (2018) with a single model. We are interested in analyzing this relationship further by experimenting with adding ELMo embeddings to models with and without syntax in order to determine whether ELMo can replace explicit syntax in SRL models, or if they can have a synergistic relationship.

4 Experimental results

In our experiments we assess the impact of replacing GLoVe embeddings (**+GloVe**) with ELMo embeddings (**+ELMo**) in strong, end-to-end neural network models for SRL: one which incorporates syntax (**LISA**) and one which does not (**SA**). The two models are identical except that the latter does not have an attention head trained to predict syntactic heads. Since the LISA model can both predict its own parses as well as consume parses from another model, as in Strubell and McCallum (2018) we experiment with providing syntactic parses from a high-quality dependency parser (**+D&M**), as well as providing the gold parses (**+Gold**) as an upper bound on the gains that can be attained by providing more accurate parses.

We compare LISA models to two baseline models: The deep bi-LSTM model of He et al. (2017) and the deep self-attention model of Tan et al. (2018). Though both also report ensemble scores, we compare to the single-model scores of both works. We note that Tan et al. (2018) is not directly comparable because they use gold predicates at test time. Despite this handicap, our best models obtain higher scores than Tan et al. (2018).

	WSJ Test		Brown Test	
	GLoVe	ELMo	GLoVe	ELMo
D&M	96.13	96.48	92.01	92.56
LISA	91.47	94.44	88.88	89.57

Table 1: Dependency parse accuracy (UAS) on CoNLL-2005.

4.1 Data and pre-processing

We evaluate our models on the data from the CoNLL-2005 semantic role labeling shared task (Carreras and Màrquez, 2005). This corpus annotates the WSJ portion of the Penn TreeBank corpus (Marcus et al., 1993) with semantic roles in the PropBank style (Palmer et al., 2005), plus a challenging out-of-domain test set derived from the Brown corpus (Francis and Kučera, 1964). This dataset contains only verbal predicates and 28 distinct role label types. We obtain 105 SRL labels (including continuations) after encoding predicate argument segment boundaries with BIO tags. We use Stanford syntactic dependencies v3.5.

4.2 Syntactic parsing

Table 1 presents the accuracy (UAS) of our dependency parsers. We experiment with adding ELMo embeddings to a strong graph-based dependency parser (Dozat and Manning, 2017), and present LISA's parsing accuracy with GloVe and ELMo embeddings. ELMo increases parsing accuracy in both models and both datasets, though by a much wider margin (3 points) for LISA, which attains much lower scores without ELMo. Incorporating ELMo into LISA is very beneficial to parsing accuracy, helping to close the gap between LISA and D&M parsing performance. In subsequent experiments, D&M refers to the best model in Table 1, D&M+ELMo.

4.3 Semantic role labeling

In Table 2 we present our main results on SRL. First, we see that adding ELMo embeddings increases SRL F1 across the board. The greatest gains from adding ELMo are to the SA models, which do not incorporate syntax. ELMo embeddings improve the SA models so much that they nearly close the gap between SA and LISA: with GloVe embeddings LISA obtains 1.5-2.5 more F1 points than SA, whereas with ELMo embeddings the difference is closer to 0.3 F1. This is despite ELMo embeddings increasing LISA's parse accu-

Model	Dev			WSJ Test			Brown Test		
	P	R	F	P	R	F	P	R	F
He et al. (2017)	80.3	80.4	80.3	80.2	82.3	81.2	67.6	69.6	68.5
Tan et al. (2018)†	82.6	**83.6**	83.1	84.5	**85.2**	84.8	73.5	**74.6**	74.1
SA+GloVe	78.54	76.90	77.71	81.43	80.69	81.06	70.10	66.01	67.99
LISA+GloVe	81.25	80.03	80.64	82.78	82.57	82.68	71.93	69.45	70.67
+D&M	82.68	82.12	82.40	84.12	83.92	84.02	73.96	70.97	72.43
+*Gold*	*86.02*	*85.11*	*85.56*	—	—	—	—	—	—
SA+ELMo	83.67	82.37	83.02	84.29	83.95	84.12	73.76	71.02	72.36
LISA+ELMo	84.18	82.71	83.44	84.62	84.24	84.43	73.70	71.70	72.69
+D&M	**84.56**	83.29	**83.92**	**85.40**	84.93	**85.17**	**75.27**	73.40	**74.33**
+*Gold*	*87.56*	*86.01*	*86.77*	—	—	—	—	—	—

Table 2: Precision, recall and F1 on CoNLL-2005 with predicted predicates. † denotes that models were evaluated on gold predicates.

racy by 3 points on the WSJ test set (Table 1). These results suggest that ELMo does model syntax in some way, or at least the model is able to leverage ELMo embeddings about as well as LISA's predicted parses to inform its SRL decisions.

However, when we add higher-accuracy parses (+D&M) to LISA, we do see greater improvements over the syntax-agnostic model, even with ELMo embeddings. We see that incorporating explicit syntax representations is still helpful even with ELMo's strong representations. On the WSJ test set, supplying LISA with D&M parses gives about 1 point of F1 over the SA baseline, and on the out-of-domain test set, we see that the parses supply almost 2 additional points of F1 over the syntax-agnostic model. We note that with ELMo embeddings and D&M parses, LISA obtains new state-of-the-art results for a single model on this dataset *when compared to a model (Tan et al., 2018) which is given gold predicates at test time*, despite our models using predicted predicates. Our model's gains in F1 come from obtaining higher precision than Tan et al. (2018) (fewer false positives).

The explicit parse representations appear to be particularly helpful on out-of-domain data, which makes sense for two reasons: First, since the Brown test set is out-of-domain for the ELMo embeddings, we would expect them to help less on this corpus than on the in-domain WSJ text. Second, the parse trees should provide a relatively domain-agnostic signal to the model, so we would expect them to help the most in out-of-domain evaluation.

		WSJ Test		
		P	R	F
He et al. (2017)		94.5	98.5	96.4
GloVe	SA	98.27	98.14	98.20
	LISA	98.34	98.04	98.19
ELMo	SA	98.66	97.51	98.08
	LISA	98.58	97.28	97.93

		Brown Test		
		P	R	F
He et al. (2017)		89.3	95.7	92.4
GloVe	SA	94.68	92.91	93.79
	LISA	95.43	93.41	94.41
ELMo	SA	95.70	91.42	93.51
	LISA	96.46	91.54	93.94

Table 3: Predicate detection precision, recall and F1 on CoNLL-2005.

We also evaluate on the development set with gold parse trees at test time. Fairly large gains of nearly 3 F1 points can still be obtained using gold parses even with ELMo embeddings, suggesting that syntax could help even more if we could produce more accurate syntactic parses, or more specifically, the types of mistakes still made by highly accurate dependency parsers (e.g. prepositional phrase attachments) negatively impact SRL models which rely on syntax.

Table 3 lists precision, recall and F1 of our predicate detection. We note that there is very little difference in predicate detection F1 between GloVe and ELMo models, demonstrating that the differ-

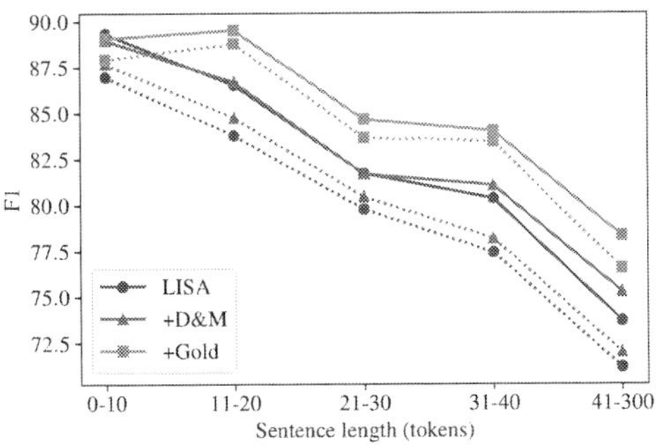

Figure 1: F1 score as a function of sentence length. Solid/dotted lines indicate ELMo/GLoVe embeddings, respectively.

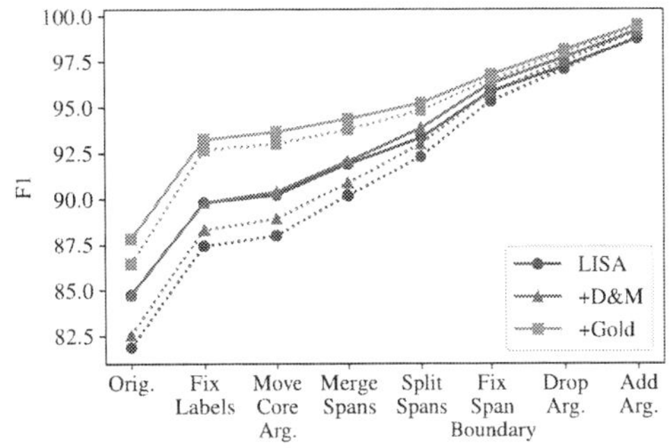

Figure 2: F1 score on CoNLL-2005 after performing incremental corrections from He et al. (2017). Solid/dotted lines indicate ELMo/GLoVe embeddings, respectively.

ence in scores can not be attributed to better predicate detection. If anything, the predicate detection scores with ELMo are slightly lower than with GloVe. We observe that in particular on the Brown test set, ELMo predicate detection precision is notably higher than GloVe while recall is lower.

4.4 Analysis

We follow Strubell and McCallum (2018) and He et al. (2017) and perform an analysis on the development dataset to ascertain which types of errors ELMo helps resolve, and how this compares with the types of errors that occur when LISA is provided with a gold parse. In Figure 1 we bucket sentences by length and plot F1 score as a function of sentence length across different models reported in Table 2. Solid lines indicate ELMo models, while dotted lines indicate models trained with GloVe. For GloVe models, we see that models without gold parses maintain about the same difference in F1 across all sentence lengths, while the gold parse obtains significant advantages for sentence lengths greater than 10. With ELMo embeddings, the relationship between models with gold and predicted parses remains the same, but interestingly the LISA and D&M parses obtain the same scores through sentence lengths 21-30, then diverge more as sentences get longer. This trend suggests that while the ELMo embeddings help LISA parse shorter sentences, up to length 30, the D&M model trained specifically on parsing is more accurate on longer sentences. This could be indicative of ELMo's ability to model long-range dependencies.

In Figure 2 we follow the analysis from He et al. (2017) which bins SRL errors into 7 different error types,[5] then incrementally fixes each error type in order to better understand which error types contribute most to SRL errors. We follow Strubell and McCallum (2018) and compare these errors across models with access to different levels of parse information, and which are trained with GloVe and ELMo word representations. As in Figure 1, solid lines in Figure 2 represent models trained with ELMo embeddings and the dashed lines indicate models trained with GloVe.

The overall trend is that supplying the gold parse helps most with segment boundary mistakes, i.e. those resolved by merging or splitting predicted role spans, for both ELMo and GloVe models. The ELMo models clearly begin to close the gap between models given predicted and gold parses by making less of these boundary mistakes, which is not simply due to better parse accuracy since the GlovE+D&M model has access to the same parses as ELMo+D&M.

5 Conclusion

To address the question of whether syntax is still relevant in SRL models with tokens embedded by deep, unsupervised, sentence-aware models such as ELMo, we compared the performance of LISA, a syntactically-informed SRL model, trained with ELMo and GloVe token representations. We found that although these representations improve LISA's parsing and SRL tagging performance substantially, models trained to leverage syntax still obtain better F1 than models without syntax even

[5]Refer to He et al. (2017) for more detailed descriptions of the error types

when provided with ELMo embeddings, especially on out-of-domain data. We conclude that syntax is indeed still relevant in neural architectures for SRL. In future work, we are interested in exploring similar analysis for NLP tasks which have less obvious ties to syntactic structure.

Acknowledgments

We thank Luheng He for providing her excellent error analysis scripts, Timothy Dozat and the authors of tensor2tensor for releasing their code, Daniel Andor and David Weiss for helpful discussions, and the reviewers for their thoughtful comments. This work is supported in part by the Center for Data Science and the Center for Intelligent Information Retrieval, in part by the Chan Zuckerberg Initiative under the project "Scientific Knowledge Base Construction," and in part by an IBM PhD Fellowship Award to ES. Any opinions, findings and conclusions or recommendations expressed in this material are those of the authors and do not necessarily reflect those of the sponsor.

References

Xavier Carreras and Lluís Màrquez. 2005. Introduction to the conll-2005 shared task: Semantic role labeling. In *CoNLL*.

Rich Caruana. 1993. Multitask learning: a knowledge-based source of inductive bias. In *ICML*.

Ciprian Chelba, Tomas Mikolov, Mike Schuster, Qi Ge, Thorsten Brants, Phillipp Koehn, and Tony Robinson. 2014. One billion word benchmark for measuring progress in statistical language modeling. In *INTERSPEECH*. pages 2635–2639.

Ronan Collobert, Jason Weston, Léon Bottou, Michael Karlen, Koray Kavukcuoglu, and Pavel Kuksa. 2011. Natural language processing (almost) from scratch. *Journal of Machine Learning Research* 12(Aug):2493–2537.

Timothy Dozat and Christopher D. Manning. 2017. Deep biaffine attention for neural dependency parsing. In *ICLR*.

Nicholas FitzGerald, Oscar Täckström, Kuzman Ganchev, and Dipanjan Das. 2015. Semantic role labeling with neural network factors. In *Proceedings of the 2015 Conference on Empirical Methods in Natural Language Processing*. pages 960–970.

W. N. Francis and H. Kučera. 1964. Manual of information to accompany a standard corpus of present-day edited american english, for use with digital computers. Technical report, Department of Linguistics, Brown University, Providence, Rhode Island.

Luheng He, Kenton Lee, Mike Lewis, and Luke Zettlemoyer. 2017. Deep semantic role labeling: What works and whats next. In *Proceedings of the 55th Annual Meeting of the Association for Computational Linguistics*.

Richard Johansson and Pierre Nugues. 2008. Dependency-based semantic role labeling of propbank. In *Proceedings of the 2008 Conference on Empirical Methods in Natural Language Processing*. pages 69–78.

John D. Lafferty, Andrew McCallum, and Fernando C. N. Pereira. 2001. Conditional random fields: Probabilistic models for segmenting and labeling sequence data. In *Proceedings of the Eighteenth International Conference on Machine Learning (ICML)*. pages 282–289.

Kenton Lee, Luheng He, Mike Lewis, and Luke Zettlemoyer. 2017. End-to-end neural coreference resolution. In *Proceedings of the 2017 Conference on Empirical Methods in Natural Language Processing*. Association for Computational Linguistics, pages 188–197. http://aclweb.org/anthology/D17-1018.

Mike Lewis, Luheng He, and Luke Zettlemoyer. 2015. Joint A* CCG Parsing and Semantic Role Labeling. In *EMNLP*.

Xuezhe Ma and Eduard Hovy. 2016. End-to-end sequence labeling via bi-directional lstm-cnns-crf. In *Proceedings of the 54th Annual Meeting of the Association for Computational Linguistics*. page 10641074.

Diego Marcheggiani, Anton Frolov, and Ivan Titov. 2017. A simple and accurate syntax-agnostic neural model for dependency-based semantic role labeling. In *CoNLL*.

Diego Marcheggiani and Ivan Titov. 2017. Encoding sentences with graph convolutional networks for semantic role labeling. In *Proceedings of the 2017 Conference on Empirical Methods in Natural Language Processing (EMNLP)*.

Mitchell P. Marcus, Mary Ann Marcinkiewicz, and Beatrice Santorini. 1993. Building a large annotated corpus of English: The Penn TreeBank. *Computational Linguistics – Special issue on using large corpora: II* 19(2):313–330.

Tomas Mikolov, Ilya Sutskever, Kai Chen, Greg Corrado, and Jeffrey Dean. 2013. Distributed representations of words and phrases and their compositionality. In *NIPS*.

Martha Palmer, Daniel Gildea, and Paul Kingsbury. 2005. The proposition bank: An annotated corpus of semantic roles. *Computational Linguistics* 31(1).

Jeffrey Pennington, Richard Socher, and Christopher D. Manning. 2014. Glove: Global vectors for word representation. In *EMNLP*.

Matthew Peters, Waleed Ammar, Chandra Bhagavatula, and Russell Power. 2017. Semi-supervised sequence tagging with bidirectional language models. In *Proceedings of the 55th Annual Meeting of the Association for Computational Linguistics (Volume 1: Long Papers)*. Association for Computational Linguistics, pages 1756–1765. https://doi.org/10.18653/v1/P17-1161.

Matthew E. Peters, Mark Neumann, Mohit Iyyer, Matt Gardner, Christopher Clark, Kenton Lee, and Luke Zettlemoyer. 2018. Deep contextualized word representations. In *NAACL*.

Sameer Pradhan, Wayne Ward, Kadri Hacioglu, James Martin, and Dan Jurafsky. 2005. Semantic role labeling using different syntactic views. In *Proceedings of the Association for Computational Linguistics 43rd annual meeting (ACL)*.

Vasin Punyakanok, Dan Roth, and Wen-Tau Yih. 2008. The importance of syntactic parsing and inference in semantic role labeling. *Computational Linguistics* 34(2):257–287.

Michael Roth and Mirella Lapata. 2016. Neural semantic role labeling with dependency path embeddings. In *Proceedings of the 54th Annual Meeting of the Association for Computational Linguistics (ACL)*. pages 1192–1202.

Emma Strubell and Andrew McCallum. 2018. Linguistically-informed self-attention for semantic role labeling. https://arxiv.org/abs/1804.08199v1.

Mihai Surdeanu, Lluís Màrquez, Xavier Carreras, and Pere R. Comas. 2007. Combination strategies for semantic role labeling. *Journal of Artificial Intelligence Research* 29:105–151.

Charles Sutton and Andrew McCallum. 2005. Joint parsing and semantic role labeling. In *CoNLL*.

Oscar Täckström, Kuzman Ganchev, and Dipanjan Das. 2015. Efficient inference and structured learning for semantic role labeling. *TACL* 3:29–41.

Zhixing Tan, Mingxuan Wang, Jun Xie, Yidong Chen, and Xiaodong Shi. 2018. Deep semantic role labeling with self-attention. In *AAAI*.

Kristina Toutanova, Aria Haghighi, and Christopher D. Manning. 2008. A global joint model for semantic role labeling. *Computational Linguistics* 34(2):161–191.

Ashish Vaswani, Noam Shazeer, Niki Parmar, Jakob Uszkoreit, Llion Jones, Aidan N Gomez, Lukasz Kaiser, and Illia Polosukhin. 2017. Attention is all you need. In *31st Conference on Neural Information Processing Systems (NIPS)*.

Jie Zhou and Wei Xu. 2015. End-to-end learning of semantic role labeling using recurrent neural networks. In *Proc. of the Annual Meeting of the Association for Computational Linguistics (ACL)*.

Subcharacter Information in Japanese Embeddings: When Is It Worth It?

Marzena Karpinska[1], **Bofang Li**[2,3], **Anna Rogers**[4] **and Aleksandr Drozd**[3,5]
[1] Department of Language and Information Science, The University of Tokyo
[2] School of Information, Renmin University of China
[3] Department of Mathematical and Computing Science, Tokyo Institute of Technology
[4] Department of Computer Science, University of Massachusetts Lowell
[5] AIST- Tokyo Tech Real World Big-Data Computation Open Innovation Laboratory
karpinska@phiz.c.u-tokyo.ac.jp, libofang@ruc.edu.cn
arogers@cs.uml.edu, alex@blackbird.pw

Abstract

Languages with logographic writing systems present a difficulty for traditional character-level models. Leveraging the subcharacter information was recently shown to be beneficial for a number of intrinsic and extrinsic tasks in Chinese. We examine whether the same strategies could be applied for Japanese, and contribute a new analogy dataset for this language.

1 Introduction

No matter how big a corpus is, there will always be rare and out-of-vocabulary (OOV) words, and they pose a problem for the widely used word embedding models such as word2vec. A growing body of work on subword and character-level representations addresses this limitation in composing the representations for OOV words out of their parts (Kim et al., 2015; Zhang et al., 2015).

However, logographic writing systems consist of thousands of characters, varying in frequency in different domains. Fortunately, many Chinese characters (called *kanji* in Japanese) contain semantically meaningful components. For example, 木 (a standalone kanji for the word *tree*) also occurs as a component in 桜 (*sakura*) and 杉 (*Japanese cypress*).

We investigate the effect of explicit inclusion of kanjis and kanji components in the word embedding space on word similarity and word analogy tasks, as well as sentiment polarity classification. We show that the positive results reported for Chinese carry over to Japanese only partially, that the gains are not stable, and in many cases character ngrams perform better than character-level models. We also contribute a new large dataset for word analogies, the first one for this relatively low-resourced language, and a tokenizer-friendly version of its only similarity dataset.

2 Related Work

To date, most work on representing subcharacter information relies on language-specific resources that list character components[1]. A growing list of papers address various combinations of word-level, character-level and subcharacter-level embeddings in Chinese (Sun et al., 2014; Li et al., 2015; Yu et al., 2017). They have been successful on a range of tasks, including similarity and analogy (Yu et al., 2017; Yin et al., 2016), text classification (Li et al., 2015) sentiment polarity classification (Benajiba et al., 2017), segmentation, and POS-tagging (Shao et al., 2017).

Japanese kanjis were borrowed from Chinese, but it remains unclear whether these success stories could also carry over to Japanese. Chinese is an analytic language, but Japanese is agglutinative, which complicates tokenization. Also, in Japanese, words can be spelled either in kanji or in phonetic alphabets (*hiragana* and *katakana*), which further increases data sparsity. Numerous homonyms make this sparse data also noisy.

To the best of our knowledge, subcharacter information in Japanese has been addressed only by Nguyen et al. (2017) and Ke and Hagiwara (2017).

[1] Liu et al. (2017) showed the possibility of learning this information for any language through visual feature recognition.

Proceedings of the Workshop on the Relevance of Linguistic Structure in Neural Architectures for NLP, pages 28–37
Melbourne, Australia, July 19, 2018.

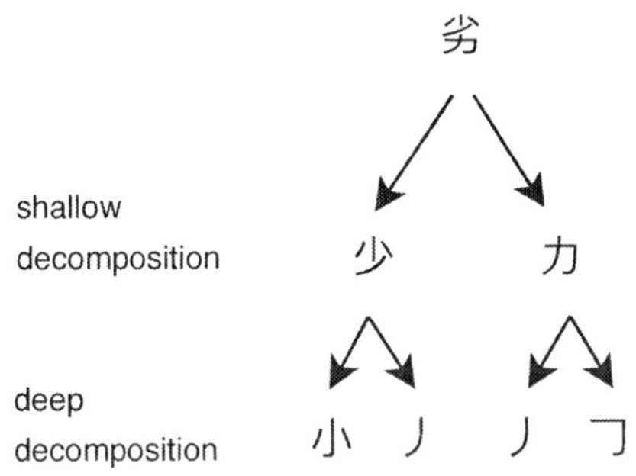

(a) Kanji decomposition levels

Original sentence:
彼は数学の天才だが、パソコンには劣る。

Shallow decomposition:
(彳 皮) 彼は (娄攵) 数 (⺍ 冖 子) 学の
(一大) 天 (才) 才だが、パソコンには (少力) 劣る。

Translation:
He is a genius at math, but will lose to a computer.

(b) Example sentence with shallow decomposition

Figure 1: Incorporating subcharacter information in Japanese

The former consider the language modeling task and compare several kinds of kanji decomposition, evaluating on model perplexity. Ke and Hagiwara (2017) propose to use subcharacter information instead of characters, showing that such a model performs on par with word and character-level models on sentiment classification, with considerably smaller vocabulary.

This study explores a model comparable to that proposed by Yu et al. (2017) for Chinese. We jointly learn a representation of words, kanjis, and kanjis' components, and we evaluate it on similarity, analogy, and sentiment classification tasks. We also contribute jBATS, the first analogy dataset for Japanese.

3 Incorporating Subcharacter Information

Kanji analysis depends on its complexity. Kanjis consisting of only 2-4 strokes may not be decomposable, or only containing 1-2 simple components (*bushu*). The more complex kanjis can usually be decomposed in analyzable bushu. This is referred to as shallow and deep decomposition (Figure 1a).

Nguyen et al. (2017) compared several decomposition databases in language modeling and concluded that shallow decomposition yields lower perplexity. This is rather to be expected, since many "atomic" bushu are not clearly meaningful. For example, Figure 1a shows the kanji 劣 ("to be inferior") as decomposable into 少 ("little, few") and 力 ("strength"). At the deep decomposition, only bushu 小 ("small") can be clearly related to the meaning of the original kanji 劣.

Hence, we use shallow decomposition. The bushu are obtained from IDS[2], a database that performed well for Nguyen et al. (2017). IDS is generated with character topic maps, which enables wider coverage[3] than crowd-sourced alternatives such as GlyphWiki.

In pre-processing each kanji was prepended the list of bushu (Figure 1b). Two corpora were used: the Japanese Wikipedia dump of April 01, 2018 and a collection of 1,859,640 Mainichi newspaper articles (Nichigai Associate, 1994-2009). We chose newspapers because this domain has a relatively higher rate of words spelled in kanji rather than hiragana.

As explained above, tokenization is not a trivial task in Japanese. The classic dictionary-based tokenizers such as MeCab or Juman, or their more recent ports such as Kuromoji do not handle OOV very well, and the newer ML-based tokenizers such as TinySegmenter or Micter are also not fully reliable. We tokenized the corpora with MeCab using a weekly updated neologism dictionary[4], which yielded roughly 357 million tokens for Mainichi and 579 for Wiki[5]. The tokenization was highly inconsistent: for example, 満腹感 ("feeling full") is split into 満腹 ("full stomach") and 感 ("feeling"), but 恐怖感 ("feeling fear") is a single word, rather than 恐怖 + 感 ("fear" and "feeling"). We additionally pre-processed the corpora to correct the tokenization for all the affixes

[2] `http://github.com/cjkvi/cjkvi-ids`

[3] A limitation of IDS is that it does not unify the representations of several frequent bushu, which could decrease the overall quality of the resulting space (e.g. 心 "heart" is being pictured as 心, 忄 and ⺗ depending on its position in kanji).

[4] `http://github.com/neologd/mecab-ipadic-neologd`

[5] The Wikipedia tokenized corpus is available at `http://vecto.space/data/corpora/ja`

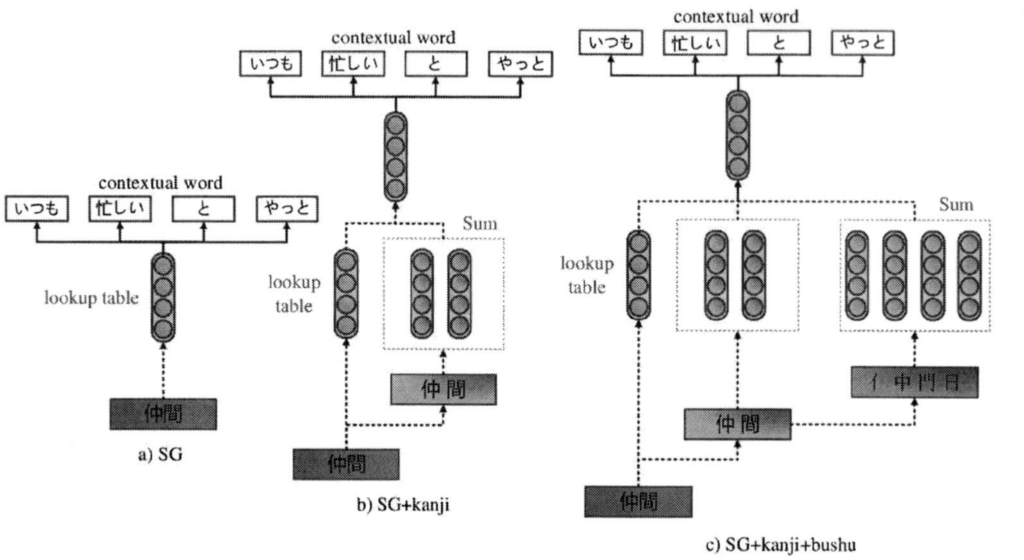

Figure 2: Model architecture of SG, SG+kanji, and SG+kanji+bushu. Example sentence: いつも 忙しい 仲間 と やっと 会え た ("I have finally met with my busy colleague."), window size 2.

in jBATS (section 5).

4 Model architecture

4.1 Baselines

Original SG. Skip-Gram (SG) (Mikolov et al., 2013) is a popular word-level model. Given a target word in the corpus, SG model uses the vector of this target word to predict its contextual words.

FastText. FastText (Bojanowski et al., 2017) is a state-of-the-art subword-level model that learns morphology from character n-grams. In this model, each word is considered as the sum of all the character n-grams.

4.2 Characters and subcharacters

Characters (*kanji*). To take individual kanji into account we modified SG by summing the target word vector w with vectors of its constituent characters c_1, and c_2. This can be regarded as a special case of FastText, where the minimal n-gram size and maximum n-gram size are both set to 1. Our model is similar to the one suggested by Yu et al. (2017), who learn Chinese word embeddings based on characters and sub-characters. We refer to this model as SG+kanji.

Subcharacters (*bushu*). Similarly to characters, we sum the vector of the target word, its constituent characters, and their constituent bushu to incorporate the bushu information. For example, Figure 3 shows that the vector of the word 仲間, the vectors of characters 仲 and 間, and the vectors of bushu 亻, 中, 門, 日 are summed to predict the contextual words. We refer to this model as SG+kanji+bushu.

Expanding vocabulary. FastText, SG+kanji and SG+kanji+bushu models can be used to compute the representation for any word as a sum of the vectors of its constituents. We collect the vocabulary of all the datasets used in this paper, calculate the vectors for any words missing in the embedding vocabulary, and add them. Such models will be referred to as MODEL+OOV.

4.3 Implementation

All models were implemented in Chainer framework (Tokui et al., 2015) with the following parameters: vector size 300, batch size 1000, negative sampling size 5, window size 2. For performance reasons all models were trained for 1 epoch. Words, kanjis and bushu appearing less than 50 times in the corpus were ignored. The optimization function was Adam (Kingma and Ba, 2014). The n-gram size of FastText[6] is set to 1, for

[6]The original FastText code[7] has some inherent differences from our Chainer implementation, as it was designed for CPU only. On each CPU thread, it directly updates the weight parameters after evaluation of each sample. To take the advantage of GPU, we use mini-batch (size 1000) to par-

	Relation	Example		Relation	Example
Inflections	I01 Verb: u-form >a-form	使う: 使わ	Lexicography	L01 hypernyms (animals)	カメ: 爬虫/脊椎動物/
	I02 Verb: u-form >o-form	受ける: 受けよ		L02 hypernyms (misc.)	椅子: 支え/器具/道具/人工物...
	I03 Verb: u-form >e-form	起きる: 起きれ		L03 hyponyms (misc.)	肉: 牛肉/牛/ビーフ/鳥肉/...
	I04 Verb: u-form >te-form	会う : 会っ		L04 meronyms (substance)	バッグ: 革/生地/布/プラスチック
	I05 Verb: a-form >o-form	書か : 書こ		L05 meronyms (member)	鳥: 群れ/家畜
	I06 Verb: o-form >e-form	歌お: 歌え		L06 meronyms (part)	アカデミア: 大学/大学院/学院...
	I07 Verb: e-form >te-form	勝て: 勝っ		L07 synonyms (intensity)	つまらない,退屈/くだらない/...
	I08 i-Adj.: i-form >ku-form	良い: 良く		L08 synonyms (exact)	赤ちゃん: 赤ん坊/ベビー
	I09 i-Adj: i-form >ta-form	良い: 良かっ		L09 antonyms (gradable)	大きい: 小さい/ちび/ちっちゃい...
	I10 i-Adj.: ku-form >ta-form	良く: 良かっ		L10 antonyms (binary)	出口: 入り口/入口
Derivation	D01 na-adj + "化"	活性: 活性化	Encyclopedia	E01 capital: country	ロンドン: イギリス/英国
	D02 i-adj + "さ"	良い: 良さ		E02 country: language	フランス : フランス語
	D03 noun + "者"	消費: 消費者		E03 jp. prefecture: city	沖縄県: 那覇/那覇市
	D04 "不" + noun	人気: 不人気		E04 name: nationality	アリストテレス: ギリシャ人
	D05 noun + "会"	運動: 運動会		E05 name: occupation	アリストテレス: 哲学者
	D06 noun/na-adj. + "感"	存在: 存在感		E06 onomatopoeia : feeling	ドキドキ: 緊張/恐怖
	D07 noun/na-adj. + "性"	可能: 可能性		E07 company: product	日産: 車/自動車
	D08 noun/na-adj. + "力"	影響: 影響力		E08 object: usage	ギター : 弾く
	D09 "大"+ noun/na-adj.	好き: 大好き		E09 polite terms	おっしゃる: 申し上げる
	D10: (in)transitive verb	起きる:起こす		E10 object: color	カラス: 黒/黒い

Table 1: jBATS: structure and examples

reliable comparison with our character model. We experimented with 1/2 of Mainichi corpus while developing the models, and then trained them on full Mainichi and Wikipedia. All sets of embeddings are available for download[8].

For SG+kanji+bushu model there were 2510 bushu in total, 1.47% of which were ignored in the model since they were not in the standard UTF-8 word ("w) encoding. This affected 1.37% of tokens in Wikipedia.

5 Evaluation: jBATS

We present jBATS[9], a new analogy dataset for Japanese that is comparable to BATS (Gladkova et al., 2016), currently the largest analogy dataset for English. Like BATS, jBATS covers 40 linguistic relations which are listed in Table 1. There are 4 types of relations: inflectional and derivational morphology, and encyclopedic and lexicographic semantics. Each type has 10 categories, with 50 word pairs per category (except for E03 which has 47 pairs, since there are only 47 prefectures). This enables generation of 97,712 analogy questions.

The inflectional morphology set is based on the traditional Japanese grammar (Teramura, 1982) which lists 7 different forms of *godan*, *shimoichidan* and *kamiichidan* verbs, as well as 5 forms of *i*-adjectives. Including the past tense form, there are 8 and 6 forms for verbs and adjectives respectively. All categories were adjusted to the MeCab tokenization. After excluding redundant or rare forms there were 5 distinctive forms for verbs and 3 for adjectives, which were paired to form 7 verb and 3 adjective categories.

The derivational morphology set includes 9 highly productive affixes which are usually represented by a single kanji character, and a set of pairs of transitive and intransitive verbs which are formed with several infix patterns.

The encyclopedic and lexicographic semantics sections were designed similarly to BATS (Gladkova et al., 2016), but adjusted for Japanese. For example, UK counties were replaced with Japanese prefectures. The E09 *animal-young* category of BATS would be rendered with a prefix in Japanese, and was replaced with plain: honorific word pairs, a concept highly relevant for the Japanese culture.

All tokens were chosen based on their frequencies in BCCWJ[10] (Maekawa, 2008), the Balanced Corpus of Contemporary Written Japanese, and the Mainichi newspaper corpus described in Section 3. We aimed to choose relatively frequent and not genre-specific words. For broader categories (adjectives and verbs) we balanced between BCCWJ and Mainichi corpora, choosing items of mean frequencies between 3,000 and 100,000

allelize training.

[8]http://vecto.space/data/embeddings/ja

[9]http://vecto.space/projects/jBATS

[10]http://pj.ninjal.ac.jp/corpus_center/bccwj/en/freq-list.html

whenever possible.

6 Results

6.1 Word similarity

The recent Japanese word similarity dataset (Sakaizawa and Komachi, 2017) contains 4,851 word pairs that were annotated by crowd workers with agreement 0.56-0.69. Like MEN (Bruni et al., 2014) and SimLex (Hill et al., 2015), this dataset is split by parts of speech: verbs, nouns, adjectives and adverbs. We refer to this dataset as jSIM.

The division by parts of speech is relevant for this study: many Japanese adverbs are written mostly in hiragana and would not benefit from bushu information. However, some pairs in jSIM were misclassified. Furthermore, since this dataset was based on paraphrases, many pairs contained phrases rather than words, and/or words in forms that would not be preserved in a corpus tokenized the Mecab style (which is the most frequently used in Japanese NLP). Therefore, for embeddings with standard pre-processing jSIM would have a very high OOV rate. The authors of jSIM do not actually present any experiments with word embeddings.

We have prepared 3 versions of jSIM that are summarized in Table 2. The *full* version contains most word pairs of the original dataset (except those which categories were ambiguous or mixed), with corrected POS attribution in 2-5% of pairs in each category[11]: for example, the pair 苛立たしい - 忌ま忌ましい was moved from verbs to adjectives. The *tokenized* version contains only the items that could be identified by a Mecab-style tokenizer, and had no more than one content-word stem: e.g. this would exclude phrases like 早く来る. However, many of the remaining items could become ambiguous when tokenized: 終わった would become 終わっ た - and 終わっ could map to 終わった, 終わって, 終わっちゃう, etc., and therefore be more difficult to detect in the similarity task. Thus we also prepared the *unambiguous* subset which contains only the words that could still be identified unambiguously even when tokenized (for example, 迷う remains 迷う). All these versions of jSIM are available for download[12].

Table 3 shows the results on all 3 datasets on all models, trained on the full Mainichi corpus, a half Mainichi corpus, and Wikipedia. The strongest effect for inclusion of bushu is observed in the OOV condition: in all datasets the Spearman's correlations are higher for SG+kanji+bushu than for other SG models, which suggests that this information is indeed meaningful and helpful. This even holds for the *full* version, where up to 90% vocabulary is missing and has to be composed. For in-vocabulary condition this effect is noticeably absent in Wikipedia (perhaps due to the higher ratio of names, where the kanji meanings are often irrelevant).

Version	Adj.	Adv.	Nouns	Verbs	Total
Original	960	902	1103	1464	4429
Full	879	893	1104	1507	4383
Tokenized	642	774	947	427	2790
Unambiguous	448	465	912	172	1997

Table 2: The size of the original and modified Japanese similarity datasets (in word pairs)

However, in most cases the improvement due to inclusion of bushu, even when it is observed, is not sufficient to catch up with the FastText algorithm, and in most cases FastText has substantial advantage. This is significant, as it might warrant the review of the previous results for Chinese on this task: of all the studies on subcharacter information in Chinese that we reviewed, only one explicitly compared their model to FastText (Benajiba et al., 2017), and their task was different (sentiment analysis).

In terms of parts of speech, the only clear effect is for the adjectives, which we attribute to the fact that many Japanese adjectives contain a single kanji character, directly related to the meaning of the word (e.g. 惜しい). The adjectives category contains 55.45% such words, compared to 14.78% for nouns and 23.71% for adverbs in the *full* jSIM (the ratio is similar for *Tokenized* and *Unambiguous* sets). On the other hand, all jSIM versions have over 70% of nouns with more than one kanji; some of them may not be directly related to the meaning of the word, and increase the noise. Ac-

[11] Division between adjectives and adverbs is problematic for the Japanese adverbial forms of adjectives, such as 安い → 安く. There were 228 such pairs in total. Since we focus on the kanji, we grouped them with the adjectives, as in the original dataset.

[12] `http://vecto.space/projects/jSIM`

Corpus	Model	Full adj	Full adv	Full noun	Full verb	Tokenized adj	Tokenized adv	Tokenized noun	Tokenized verb	Unambiguous adj	Unambiguous adv	Unambiguous noun	Unambiguous verb
Mainichi 1/2	FastText	**.366**	.190	**.331**	.355	**.392**	.285	**.333**	**.381**	.377	.232	**.328**	.337
	SG	.321	**.346**	.274	.311	.352	**.364**	.280	.341	.340	**.362**	.274	.304
	SG+kanji	.339	.290	.280	.294	.371	.330	.285	.345	.369	.305	.279	.302
	SG+kanji+bushu	.355	.300	.276	**.391**	.380	.356	.279	.375	**.384**	.326	.274	**.393**
	OOV rate per category	.659	.616	.328	.934	.506	.295	.232	.372	.462	.318	.235	.436
	FastText+OOV	**.435**	.153	**.213**	**.241**	**.416**	.185	**.259**	**.359**	**.434**	.124	**.252**	**.373**
	SG+kanji+OOV	.344	.195	.152	.210	.279	.235	.192	.307	.309	.211	.179	.327
	SG+kanji+bushu+OOV	.329	**.220**	.146	.230	.272	**.261**	.188	.318	.311	**.242**	.177	.372
Mainichi	FastText	.399	.277	**.336**	**.345**	**.436**	.296	**.337**	.355	.397	.310	**.328**	**.345**
	SG	.345	**.336**	.280	.246	.362	.333	.282	.295	.367	**.359**	.274	.246
	SG+kanji	.366	.321	.269	.334	.391	**.354**	.272	**.363**	.399	.348	.262	.334
	SG+kanji+bushu	**.405**	.318	.288	.315	.427	.311	.291	.353	**.444**	.341	.282	.315
	OOV rate per category	.582	.586	.272	.922	.389	.260	.164	.262	.384	.288	.166	.320
	FastText+OOV	**.448**	.184	**.245**	**.242**	**.438**	.222	**.286**	**.410**	**.453**	.202	**.275**	**.405**
	SG+kanji+OOV	.323	**.195**	.175	.210	.293	**.262**	.210	.353	.341	**.250**	.197	.363
	SG+kanji+bushu+OOV	.348	.171	.178	.201	.318	.231	.223	.330	.373	.249	.210	.315
Wikipedia	FastText	**.405**	.296	**.333**	**.341**	**.440**	.298	**.334**	.348	**.402**	.330	**.325**	**.341**
	SG	.309	**.298**	.299	.320	.312	.315	.299	**.382**	.307	**.345**	.296	.320
	SG+kanji	.334	**.298**	.270	.326	.331	**.327**	.275	.380	.324	.334	.271	.326
	SG+kanji+bushu	.321	.285	.282	.270	.312	.295	.287	.364	.326	.315	.279	.270
	OOV rate per category	.578	.591	.225	.909	.393	.269	.112	.192	.384	.301	.112	.203
	FastText+OOV	**.451**	**.186**	**.242**	**.243**	**.442**	.225	**.281**	**.400**	**.455**	.219	**.270**	**.402**
	SG+kanji+OOV	.296	.179	.146	.185	.240	**.240**	.191	.325	.270	.239	.184	.278
	SG+kanji+bushu+OOV	.313	.183	.159	.171	.249	.238	.208	.315	.292	**.254**	.197	.243

Table 3: Spearman's correlation with human similarity judgements. Boldface indicates the highest result on a given corpus (separately for in-vocabulary and OOV conditions). Shaded numbers indicate the highest result among the three Skip-Gram models.

cordingly, we observe the weakest effect for inclusion of bushu. However, the ratio of 1-kanji words for verbs is roughly the same as for the adjectives, but the pattern is less clear.

Adverbs are the only category in which SG clearly outperforms FastText. This could be due to a high proportion of hiragana (about 50% in all datasets), which as single-character ngrams could not yield very meaningful representations. Also, the particles と and に, important for adverbs, are lost in tokenization.

6.2 jBATS

In this paper, we consider two methods for the word analogy task. **3CosAdd** (Mikolov et al., 2013) is the original method based on linear offset between 2 vector pairs. Given an analogy a:a' :: b:b' (a is to a' as b is to b'), the answer is calculated as $b' = argmax_{\ d \in V}(cos(b', b - a + a'))$, where $cos(u, v) = \frac{u \cdot v}{||u|| \cdot ||v||}$

LRCos (Drozd et al., 2016) is a more recent and currently the best-performing method. It is based on a set of word pairs that have the same relation. For example, given a set of pairs such as *husband:wife*, *uncle:aunt*, all right-hand words are considered to be exemplars of a class ("women"), and logistic regression classifier is trained for that class. The answer (e.g. *queen*) is determined as the word vector that is the most similar to the source word (e.g. *king*), but is likely to be a *woman*:

$$b' = argmax_{\ b' \in V}(P_{\ (b' \in class)} * cos(b', b))$$

Figure 3 shows that the overall pattern of accuracy for jBATS is comparable to what Gladkova et al. (2016) report for English: derivational and inflectional morphology are much easier than either kind of semantics. In line with the results by Drozd et al. (2016), LRCos significantly outperforms 3CosAdd, achieving much better accuracy on some encyclopedic categories with which

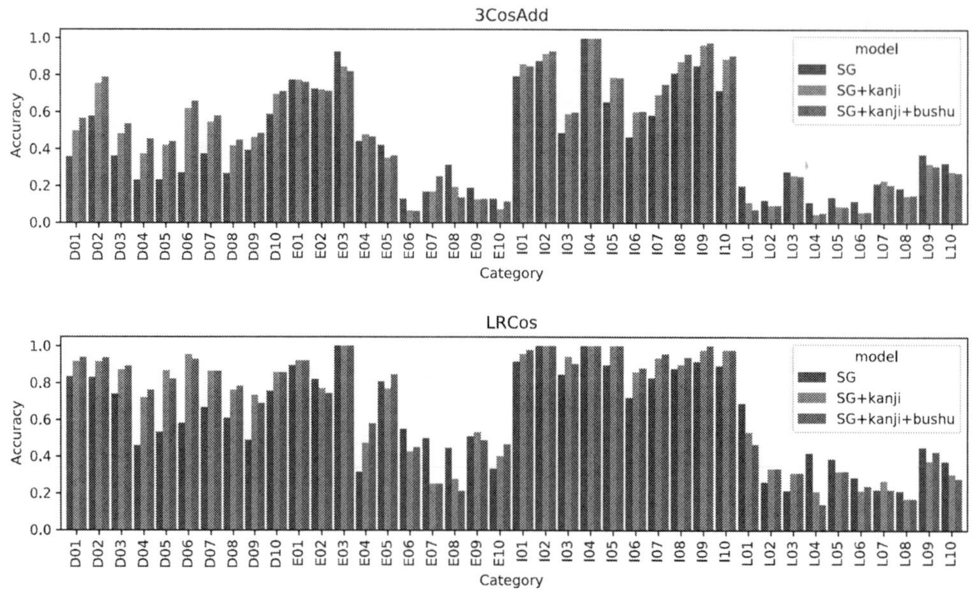

Figure 3: Accuracy on jBATS with 3CosAdd and LRCos methods (see Table 1 for the codes on x-axis).

3CosAdd does not cope at all. Lexicographic semantics is a problem, as in English, because synonyms or antonyms of different words do not constitute a coherent semantic class by themselves.

	Model	inf.	der.	enc.	lex.
Mainichi 1/2	FastText	.902	.770	.237	.075
	SG	.785	.452	**.318**	**.110**
	SG+kanji	.892	.771	.314	.102
	SG+kanji+bushu	**.912**	**.797**	.253	.083
	OOV rate per category	.070	.076	.408	.256
	FastText+OOV	.846	.758	.146	.090
	SG+kanji+OOV	.856	.747	**.181**	**.102**
	SG+kanji+bushu+OOV	**.883**	**.768**	.163	.088
Mainichi	FastText	.883	.648	.232	.093
	SG	.853	.496	**.370**	**.133**
	SG+kanji	.912	.676	.330	.123
	SG+kanji+bushu	**.926**	**.710**	.318	.118
	OOV rate per category	.022	.056	.346	.204
	FastText+OOV	.861	.746	.173	.114
	SG+kanji+OOV	**.912**	.676	**.330**	**.123**
	SG+kanji+bushu+OOV	.893	**.705**	.215	.094
Wikipedia	FastText	**.881**	.663	.242	.088
	SG	.743	.457	**.484**	**.170**
	SG+kanji	.834	.638	.422	.112
	SG+kanji+bushu	.851	**.694**	.425	.100
	OOV rate per category	.036	.060	.322	.142
	FastText+OOV	**.846**	**.750**	.158	**.127**
	SG+kanji+OOV	.794	.639	**.297**	.098
	SG+kanji+bushu+OOV	.833	.671	.293	.102

Table 4: Word analogy task accuracy (LRCos). Boldface indicates the highest result for a corpus, and the shaded numbers indicate the highest result among three Skip-Gram models.

Table 4 shows the average results per relation type for the better-performing LRCos (the pattern of results was similar for 3CosAdd). The morphology categories behave similarly to adjectives in the similarity task: the SG+kanji beats the original SG by a large margin on inflectional and derivational morphology categories, and bushu improve accuracy even further. In this task, these models also win over FastText. However, these are the categories in which the words either contain a single kanji, or (in derivational morphology) a single kanji affix needs to be identified. Semantic categories contain a variety of nouns, mostly consisting of several kanjis with various morphological patterns. Moreover, many proper nouns as well as animal species are written in katakana, with no kanjis at all. This could be the reason why information from kanjis and bushu are not helpful or even detrimental in the semantic questions.

There is a clear corpus effect in that the encyclopedic semantic questions are (predictably) more successful with Wikipedia than with Mainichi, but at the expense of morphology. This could be interpreted as confirmation of the dependence of the current analogy methods on similarity (Rogers et al., 2017): all words cannot be close to all other words, so a higher ratio of some relation type has

Error type	Example	Predicted	Percentage
correct stem, wrong form	買う : 買え :: 借りる : [借りれ]	借り	28.0%
same semantic category	アメリカ : 英語 :: イラン : [ペルシア語]	トルコ語	25.0%
antonym, correct form	深い : 深さ :: 低い : [低さ]	高さ	10.0%
antonym, wrong form	面白い : 面白さ :: 高い : [高さ]	低い	3.0%
related to target pair	アンドラ :　カタルーニャ語 :: アメリカ : [英語]	米国	8.5%
wrong stem, correct form	持つ : 持て :: 借りる : [借りれ]	買え	5.5%
duplicated token	もらう : あげる :: 内（うち）: [外]	うち	5.0%
synonym, correct form	悪い : 悪さ :: すごい : [すごさ]	器用さ	1.0%
synonym, wrong form	ほしい : ほしさ :: 固い : [固さ]	堅い	1.5%
orthography related	減る : 増える :: オン : [オフ]	フォー	1.0%
related to the source pair	前 : 次 :: 内 : [外]	下記	0.5%
alternative spelling	イスラエル : ヘブライ語 :: イラン : [ペルシア語]	ペルシャ語	0.5%
unrelated	痛い : 痛さ :: 大きい : [大きさ]	仮種皮	10.5%

Table 5: jBATS: error analysis.

to come with a decrease in some other.

6.3 Sentiment analysis

The binary sentiment classification accuracy was tested with the Rakuten reviews dataset by Zhang and LeCun (2017). Although Benajiba et al. (2017) report that incorporating subcharacter information provided a boost in accuracy on this task in Chinese, we did not confirm this to be the case for Japanese. Table 6 [13] shows that the accuracy for all models ranged between 0.92-0.93 (consistent with the results of Zhang and LeCun (2017)), so no model had a clear advantage.

Model	Main.1/2	Mainichi	Wiki
FastText	.919	.921	.920
SG	**.921**	.920	**.921**
SG+kanji	**.921**	**.924**	.919
SG+kanji+bushu	.918	.920	**.921**
OOV rate per category	.220	.220	.212
FastText+OOV	.926	.927	**.922**
SG+kanji+OOV	**.929**	**.930**	**.922**
SG+kanji+bushu+OOV	.925	.927	**.922**

Table 6: Sentiment analysis accuracy

The lack of positive effect for inclusion of kanji and bushu is to be expected, as we found that most of the dataset is written informally, in hiragana, even for words that are normally written with kanjis. Once again, this shows that the results of incorporating (sub)character information in Japanese are not the same as in Chinese, and depend on the task and domain of the texts.

Interestingly, the accuracy is just as high for all OOV models, even though about 20% of the vocabulary had to be constructed.

7 Discussion

7.1 Error analysis

We conducted manual analysis of 200 mispredictions of 3CosAdd method in I03, D02, E02 and L10 categories (50 examples in each). The percentage of different types of errors is shown in Table 5. Overall, most mistakes are interpretable, and only 10.5% of mispredicted vectors are not clearly related to the source words.

The most frequent example of mis-classification was predicting the wrong form but with the correct stem, especially in morphological categories. This is consistent with what Drozd et al. (2016) report for English and was especially frequent in the I03 and D02 categories (76% and 36% of errors per category respectively). It is not surprising since these categories consist of verbs (I03) and adjectives (D02). Furthermore, in 25% of cases the assigned item was from the same semantic category (for example, colours) and in 13% of case an antonym was predicted. Other, though relatively less frequent mistakes include semantic relations like predicting synonyms of the given word, words (or single kanji) related to either target or source pair, or simply returning the same token. Words which were not related in any way to any source word were very rare.

7.2 Vector neighborhoods

Table 7 shows that the shared semantic space of words, kanjis and bushu is indeed shared. For example, the bushu 疒 (*yamaidare* "the roof from illness") is often used in kanjis which are related to a disease. Therefore kanji like 症 ("disease") would,

[13] The Chainer framework (Tokui et al., 2015) is used to implement the CNN classifier with default settings.

疒 *yamaidare* (the roof from illness)	豸 *najina-hen* (devine beast, insect without legs)
患(sickness) 症(disease) 妊 (pregnancy) 臓 (internal organs, bowels) 腫 (tumor)	争(to fight, to compete) 蝶(butterfly) 皃(shape) 貌(shape, silhouette) 豹(leopard)
インフルエザ (influenza) 関節リウマチ (articular rheumatism) リューマチ (rheumatism) リウマチ(rheumatism) メタボリックシンドローム (metabolic syndrome)	獅子 (lion, king of beasts) 同流 (same origin, same school) 本性(true nature, human nature) 弥勒(Maitreya Buddha) 無頼 (villain, scoundrel)

Table 7: Example bushu: closest single kanji (upper row) and multiple kanji/katakana (lower row) for SG+kanji+bushu model.

of course, be similar to 疒 in the vector space. Interestingly, we also find that its close neighbors include kanjis that do not have this bushu, but are related to disease, such as 腫 and 患. Furthermore, even words written only in katakana, like インフルエザ, are correctly positioned in the same space. Similar observations can be made for bushu 豸 (*mujina-hen*) which represents a divine beast, insects without legs, animals with long spine, or a legendary Chinese beast *Xiezhi*.

7.3 Stability of the similarity results

Our similarity experiments showed that in many cases the gain of any one model over the other is not very significant and would not be reproduced in a different run and/or a different corpus. This could be due to skewed frequency distribution or the general instability of embeddings for rare words, recently demonstrated for word2vec (Wendlandt et al., 2018).

One puzzling observation is that sometimes the smaller corpus yielded better embeddings. Intuitively, the larger the corpus, the more informative distributional representations can be obtained. However, Table 3 shows that for adverbs and verbs the *full* and *tokenized* versions of jSIM a half of Mainichi was actually significantly better than the full Mainichi. It is not clear whether it is due to a lucky random initialization or some other factors.

8 Conclusion

This study presented the first evaluation of subcharacter-level distributional representations of Japanese on similarity, analogy and sentiment classification tasks. We show that the success of this approach in Chinese is transferable to Japanese only partly, but it does improve the performance of Skip-Gram model in kanji-rich domains and for tasks relying on mostly single-kanji vocabulary or morphological patterns. The effect may be stronger with a better sent of model hyperparameters, which we have not explored here, or in some other task. However, in our experiments we found that even enhanced Skip-Gram was consistently inferior to single-character ngram FastText, which has not been used as a baseline in most work on Chinese subcharacter-level embeddings.

We also contribute jBATS, the first analogy dataset for this relatively low-resourced language, and a revision of its only similarity dataset that can now be used with standard tokenized corpora. All models, datasets and embeddings are available in the `Vecto`[14] library.

Acknowledgments

This work was partially supported by JSPS KAKENHI Grant No. JP17K12739, JST CREST Grant No. JPMJCR1687 and National Natural Science Foundation of China Grant No.61472428.

References

Yassine Benajiba, Or Biran, Zhiliang Weng, Yong Zhang, and Jin Sun. 2017. The Sentimental Value of Chinese Sub-Character Components. In *Proceedings of the 9th SIGHAN Workshop on Chinese Language Processing*, pages 21–29, Taipei, Taiwan, December 1, 2017. Association for Computational Linguistics.

Piotr Bojanowski, Edouard Grave, Armand Joulin, and Tomas Mikolov. 2017. Enriching word vectors with subword information. *Transactions of the Association for Computational Linguistics*, 5:135–146.

Elia Bruni, Nam-Khanh Tran, and Marco Baroni. 2014. Multimodal distributional semantics. *J. Artif. Intell. Res.(JAIR)*, 49(2014):1–47.

Aleksandr Drozd, Anna Gladkova, and Satoshi Matsuoka. 2016. Word embeddings, analogies, and machine learning: Beyond king - man + woman = queen. In *Proceedings of COLING 2016, the 26th International Conference on Computational Linguistics: Technical Papers*, pages 3519–3530, Osaka, Japan, December 11-17.

[14] `http://vecto.space`

Anna Gladkova, Aleksandr Drozd, and Satoshi Matsuoka. 2016. Analogy-based detection of morphological and semantic relations with word embeddings: What works and what doesn't. In *Proceedings of the NAACL-HLT SRW*, pages 47–54, San Diego, California, June 12-17, 2016. ACL.

Felix Hill, Roi Reichart, and Anna Korhonen. 2015. Simlex-999: Evaluating semantic models with (genuine) similarity estimation. *Computational Linguistics*, 41(4):665–695.

Yuanzhi Ke and Masafumi Hagiwara. 2017. Radical-level Ideograph Encoder for RNN-based Sentiment Analysis of Chinese and Japanese. *arXiv:1708.03312 [cs]*.

Yoon Kim, Yacine Jernite, David Sontag, and Alexander M Rush. 2015. Character-aware neural language models. *arXiv preprint arXiv:1508.06615*.

Diederik P Kingma and Jimmy Ba. 2014. Adam: A method for stochastic optimization. *arXiv preprint arXiv:1412.6980*.

Yanran Li, Wenjie Li, Fei Sun, and Sujian Li. 2015. Component-enhanced Chinese character embeddings. In *Proceedings of the 2015 Conference on Empirical Methods in Natural Language Processing*, pages 829–834, Lisbon, Portugal, 17-21 September 2015. Association for Computational Linguistics.

Frederick Liu, Han Lu, Chieh Lo, and Graham Neubig. 2017. Learning Character-level Compositionality with Visual Features. pages 2059–2068. Association for Computational Linguistics.

Kikuo Maekawa. 2008. Compilation of the Balanced Corpus of Contemporary Written Japanese in the KOTONOHA Initiative. In *Universal Communication, 2008. ISUC'08. Second International Symposium On*, pages 169–172. IEEE.

Tomas Mikolov, Ilya Sutskever, Kai Chen, Gregory S. Corrado, and Jeffrey Dean. 2013. Distributed representations of words and phrases and their compositionality. In *NIPS*, pages 3111–3119.

Viet Nguyen, Julian Brooke, and Timothy Baldwin. 2017. Sub-character Neural Language Modelling in Japanese. In *Proceedings of the First Workshop on Subword and Character Level Models in NLP*, pages 148–153.

Nichigai Associate. 1994-2009. CD-Mainichi Shimbun de-ta shu (1994-2009).

Anna Rogers, Aleksandr Drozd, and Bofang Li. 2017. The (Too Many) Problems of Analogical Reasoning with Word Vectors. In *Proceedings of the 6th Joint Conference on Lexical and Computational Semantics (* SEM 2017)*, pages 135–148.

Yuya Sakaizawa and Mamoru Komachi. 2017. Construction of a Japanese Word Similarity Dataset. In *Proceedings of the Eleventh International Conference on Language Resources and Evaluation (LREC 2018)*, Miyazaki, Japan. European Language Resources Association (ELRA).

Yan Shao, Christian Hardmeier, Jorg Tiedemann, and Joakim Nivre. 2017. Character-based Joint Segmentation and POS Tagging for Chinese using Bidirectional RNN-CRF. page 11.

Yaming Sun, Lei Lin, Nan Yang, Zhenzhou Ji, and Xiaolong Wang. 2014. Radical-Enhanced Chinese Character Embedding. In *Neural Information Processing*, Lecture Notes in Computer Science, pages 279–286. Springer, Cham.

Hideo Teramura. 1982. *Nihongo no shintakusu to imi (Japanese syntax and meaning)*. Kuroshio Shuppan.

Seiya Tokui, Kenta Oono, Shohei Hido, and Justin Clayton. 2015. Chainer: a next-generation open source framework for deep learning. In *Proceedings of workshop on machine learning systems (LearningSys) in the twenty-ninth annual conference on neural information processing systems (NIPS)*, volume 5.

Laura Wendlandt, Jonathan K. Kummerfeld, and Rada Mihalcea. 2018. Factors Influencing the Surprising Instability of Word Embeddings. *arXiv:1804.09692 [cs]*.

Rongchao Yin, Quan Wang, Peng Li, Rui Li, and Bin Wang. 2016. Multi-Granularity Chinese Word Embedding. pages 981–986. Association for Computational Linguistics.

Jinxing Yu, Xun Jian, Hao Xin, and Yangqiu Song. 2017. Joint Embeddings of Chinese Words, Characters, and Fine-grained Subcharacter Components. pages 286–291. Association for Computational Linguistics.

Xiang Zhang and Yann LeCun. 2017. Which Encoding is the Best for Text Classification in Chinese, English, Japanese and Korean? *arXiv preprint arXiv:1708.02657*.

Xiang Zhang, Junbo Zhao, and Yann LeCun. 2015. Character-level convolutional networks for text classification. In *NIPS*, pages 649–657.

A neural parser as a direct classifier for head-final languages

Hiroshi Kanayama **Masayasu Muraoka** **Ryosuke Kohita**
IBM Research
Tokyo, Japan
{hkana, mmuraoka}@jp.ibm.com, Ryosuke.Kohita1@ibm.com

Abstract

This paper demonstrates a neural parser implementation suitable for consistently head-final languages such as Japanese. Unlike the transition- and graph-based algorithms in most state-of-the-art parsers, our parser directly selects the head word of a dependent from a limited number of candidates. This method drastically simplifies the model so that we can easily interpret the output of the neural model. Moreover, by exploiting grammatical knowledge to restrict possible modification types, we can control the output of the parser to reduce specific errors without adding annotated corpora. The neural parser performed well both on conventional Japanese corpora and the Japanese version of Universal Dependency corpus, and the advantages of distributed representations were observed in the comparison with the non-neural conventional model.

1 Introduction

Dependency parsing helps a lot to give intuitive relationships between words such as noun-verb and adjective-noun combinations. Those outputs are consumed in text mining systems (Nasukawa and Nagano, 2001) and rule-based approaches such as in fine-grained sentiment extractors (Kanayama et al., 2004), though some of recent end-to-end systems do not require intermediate parsing structures.

Many recent dependency parsers have been implemented with neural net (NN) methods with (typically bidirectional) LSTM and distributed word vectors (Dozat et al., 2017; Shi et al., 2017), as we can see in the 2017 shared task on dependency parsing from raw text for 49 languages (Zeman et al., 2017) based on the multilingual corpora of Universal Dependencies (UD) (Nivre et al., 2015).

Most of such dependency parsers exploit a transition-based algorithm (Nivre et al., 2007), a graph-based algorithm (McDonald et al., 2005) or a combination of both (Nivre and McDonald, 2008). Those algorithms addressed several problems in multilingual dependency analysis such as bidirectional dependency relationships and non-projective sentences. However, it is hard to intuitively interpret the actions to be trained on the transition-based parser. Though it can handle the history of past parsing actions, the output may violate syntactic constraints due to the limitation of visible histories. The graph-based approach captures global information in a sentence, but the difficulty in reflecting the interaction of attachment decisions causes contradictory labels in a tree.

The parsing results from the participants in the 2017 shared task show low scores on Japanese (67 to 82% in the UAS scores, excluding the team that provided the data) in particular, which shows that the language-universal approaches do not work effectively for Japanese.[1]

The syntactic structures in the Japanese version of Universal Dependencies (Tanaka et al., 2016; Asahara et al., 2018) have dependencies in both directions, as well as in other languages, since it is based on the word level annotations and the content-head dependency schema. However, when the syntactic structures are expressed with the dependencies between phrasal units (so-called *bunsetsus* in Japanese; 'PU' hereafter in this paper), the head element always comes in the right position, since Japanese is a consistently head-final language. This allows us to apply a method for such languages to simplify the model. We con-

[1]Note that another factor in the low score was the inconsistent tokenization (84 to 93% F1 value).

Proceedings of the Workshop on the Relevance of Linguistic Structure in Neural Architectures for NLP, pages 38–46
Melbourne, Australia, July 19, 2018.

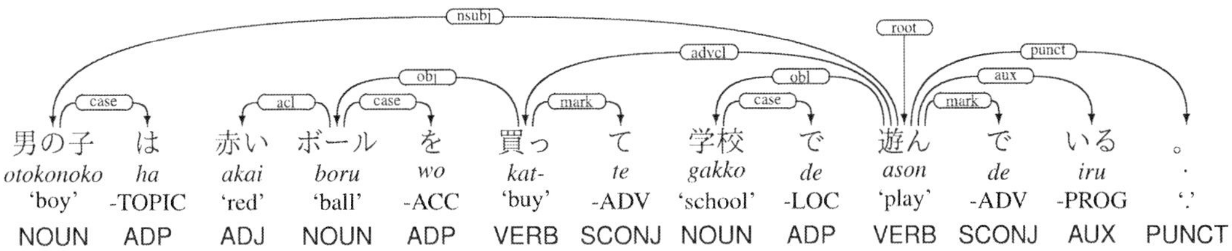

Figure 1: Japanese word-level dependencies in the UD-style content-head schema for an example sentence "男の子は赤いボールを買って学校で遊んでいる。" ('A boy bought a red ball and is playing at the school') .

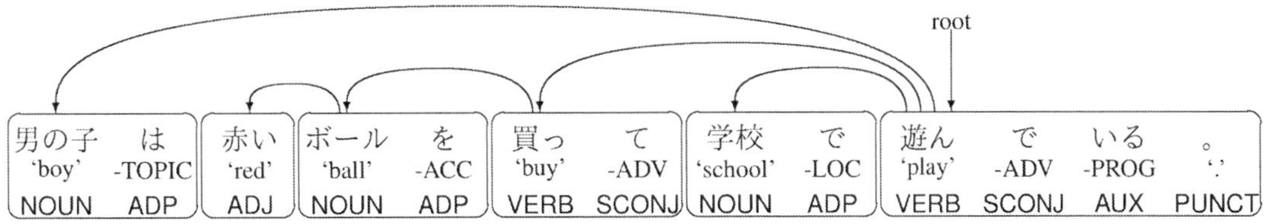

Figure 2: Japanese dependencies in PUs (phrasal units). There is a strict head-final constraint.

structed a neural parsing model to directly select the head word among the limited candidates. The model works as a classifier that outputs intuitive and consistent results while exploiting grammatical knowledge.

Section 2 reviews the head-final property of Japanese and the Triplet/Quadruplet Model (Kanayama et al., 2000) to exploit syntactic knowledge in a machine-learning parser. Section 3 designs our neural model relying on the grammatical knowledge, and its experimental results are reported in Section 4. Other head-final languages are discussed in Section 5 and some related approaches are discussed in Section 6. Section 7 concludes this paper.

2 Background

First, Section 2.1 shows the head-final property of the Japanese language. and Sections 2.2 and 2.3 explain the main ideas in the Triplet/Quadruplet Model: the methods of simplification of dependency parsing task using the linguistic knowledge.

2.1 Head-final structure in Japanese

Figure 1 shows an example of a word-level dependency structure of a Japanese sentence in the representation of Universal Dependencies. Traditionally Japanese dependency parsers have been evaluated on the unit of *bunsetsu*, a phrasal unit (PU), as performed in Kyoto University Text Corpus (Kawahara et al., 2002). A PU consists of a content word[2] and optional functional words and prefixes and suffixes. Figure 2 depicts the dependency structure represented in PUs, where the all dependencies are in a single direction. The head PU is always in the right and the rightmost PU is always the root, as long as exceptional inversion cases are not cared. In this paper we exploit this property to apply a simplified parsing algorithm: the parsing can be regarded as the selection of the head PU from the limited number of candidates PUs located to the right of the dependent in question. For example, the second PU "赤い" ('red') in Figure 2 must modify one of the four PUs from the third "ボール を" ('ball'-ACC) to the sixth PU "遊ん で いる" ('play'-PROG). The correct head is "ボール を" ('ball'-ACC).

2.2 Restriction of modification candidates

The head-final feature can further simplify the dependency parsing by adding syntactic constraints. The *Triplet/Quadruplet Model* (Kanayama et al., 2000) has been proposed to achieve the statistical dependency parsing making most of the linguistic knowledge and heuristics. In their work, a small number (about 50) of hand-crafted grammar rules determine whether a PU can modify each PU to its right in a sentence as shown in Table 1. In the rules, the modified PUs are determined on the conditions of the rightmost morpheme in the modifier PU. In addition to PoS-level relationships,

[2]In case of compound nouns and verbs, multiple content words may be included in a single PU.

Rightmost morpheme of the modifier PU	Conditions for the modified PUs
postpositional "を" *wo* (accusative)	verb, adjective
postpositional "から" *kara* ('from')	verb, adjective
postpositional "から" *kara* ('from')	nominal followed by postpositonal "まで" *made* ('to')
proper noun + postpositional "から "	proper noun followed by postpositional "の" (-GEN)
postpositional "の" *no* (genitive, nominative)	noun, verb, adjective
postpositional "と" *to* (conjunctive)	noun, verb, adjective
postpositional "と" *to* (conjunctive)	adverb "一緒に" *isshoni* ('together')
adverb	verb, adjective, adverb, nominal with copula

Table 1: The excerpt of Japanese grammar rules. The left side is the condition of the modifier PU specified with the rightmost morpheme (except for punctuation) with optional preceding morphemes, and the right side is the list of the condition for the modifiable PUs specified with the head word and optional functional words.

# of candidates	Ratio	1st	2nd	Last	Sum
1	32.7	100.0	–	–	100.0
2	28.1	74.3	26.7	–	100.0
3	17.5	70.6	12.6	16.8	100.0
4	9.9	70.4	11.1	13.8	95.3
≥5	11.8	70.2	11.1	10.5	91.9
Total	100	–	–	–	98.6

Table 2: Percentages of the position of the correct modified PU among the candidate PUs selected by the initial grammar rules. The column 'Sum' shows the coverage of the 1st, 2nd and last (the farthest) PUs in the distance from the modifier PUs. The EDR Japanese corpus was used in this analysis.

detailed condition with specific functional words and exceptional content words are covered in the rules. Even with these simplified rules, 98.5% of the modifications between PUs are covered.

The role of the grammar rules is to maximize the coverage, and the rules are simply describing high-level syntactic dependencies so that the rules can be created easily without worrying about precision or contradictory rules. The statistical information is later used to select the rules necessary for a given sentence to produce an accurate parsing result.

Furthermore, an analysis of the EDR corpus shows that 98.6% of the correct dependencies are either the nearest PU, the second nearest PU, or the farthest PU from the modifier (more details in Table 2) among the modifiable PUs enumerated by the grammar rules. Therefore, the model can be simplified by restricting the candidates to these two or three candidates and by ignoring the other PUs with a small sacrifice (1.4%) of parsing accuracy. Retaining the farthest modifiable PU from the modifier, the long distance dependencies are captured.

2.3 Calculation of modification probabilities

Let u be a modifier PU in question, c_{un} the u's n-th modification candidate PU, Φ_u and $\Psi_{c_{un}}$ the respective attributes of u and c_{un}. Then the probability of u modifying its n-th candidate is calculated by the triplet equation (1) when u has two candidates or the quadruplet equation (2) when u has three candidates.[3] These two equations are known as the Triplet and Quadruplet Model.

$$P(u \leftarrow c_{un}) = P(n \mid \Phi_u, \Psi_{c_{u1}}, \Psi_{c_{u2}}) \qquad (1)$$

$$P(u \leftarrow c_{un}) = P(n \mid \Phi_u, \Psi_{c_{u1}}, \Psi_{c_{u2}}, \Psi_{c_{u3}}) \qquad (2)$$

Assuming the independence of those modifications, the probability of the dependency tree for an entire sentence $P(T)$ is calculated as the product of the probabilities of all of the dependencies in the sentence using beam search from the rightmost PU to the left, to maximize $P(T)$ under the constraints of the projected structure.

$$P(T) \simeq \prod_u P(u \leftarrow c_{un}) \qquad (3)$$

Equations (1) and (2) have two major advantages. First, all the attributes of the modifier and its candidates can be handled simultaneously – the model expresses the context through the combination of those attributes. Second, the probability of each modification is calculated based on the

[3]It is trivial to show that $P(u \leftarrow cu_1) = 1$, when u has only one candidate.

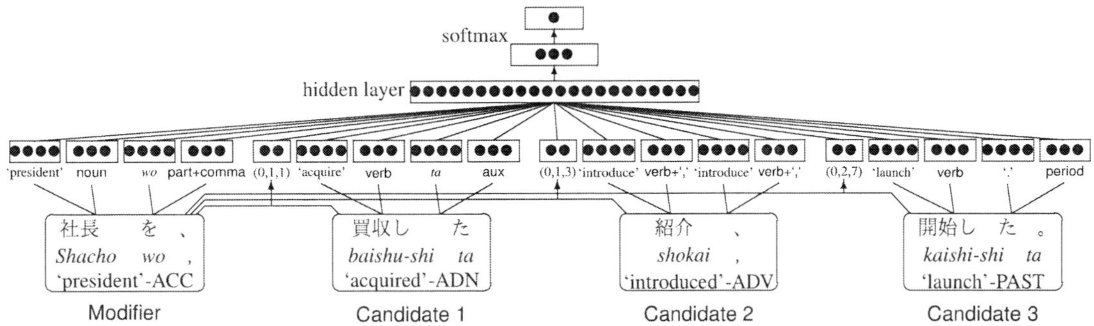

Figure 3: The neural net for the quadruplet model to select the head of the PU "社長を" ('president'-ACC) from three modification candidates in an example sentence "… 以前の社長を、$_0$買収した$_1$ 企業に紹介、$_2$ … 事業を開始した。$_3$" ('... introduced$_2$ the previous president$_0$ to the acquired$_1$ company, and launched$_3$ a ... business'). The attributes of the modifier PU and three modification candidates, and the features between the modifier and each candidate are input as distributed vectors.

relative positions of the candidates, instead of the distance from the modifier PU in the surface sentence, making the model more robust.

3 NN parsing model

In the past implementation of the parser by the Triplet/Quadruplet model (Kanayama et al., 2000), the equations (1) and (2) were calculated with logistic regression (maximum entropy method) in which many binary features represent the attributes of each PU. We designed the NN model using distributed representation of words and parts-of-speech as Chen and Manning (2014) did.

Figure 3 shows the neural net model that directly selects the head PU and an example sentence. Here, the head of "社長を" ('president-ACC') is predicted among three modification candidates selected by the method described in Section 2.2. The second candidate PU "紹介、" ('introduced-ADV') is the correct head.

To make the prediction, the attributes for each PU are extracted, and we focus on two words in a PU: the head word – the rightmost content word in the PU – and the form word – the rightmost functional word in the PU except for a punctuation. First, the surface form and the PoS of the head word and the form word are converted into vector representations. That is, two vectors are used for 6 PUs in the triplet model and 8 PUs are used in the quadruplet model. Furthermore, the following attributes between two PUs are added.

- the number of a postpositional "は *ha*"[4] between two PUs (0, 1, 2, 3, 4, or 5+)
- the number of commas between two PUs (0, 1, 2, 3, 4, or 5+)
- the distance between two PUs (1, 2, 3, ..., 9, or 10+)

These features expressed as vectors are concatenated to form a single layer, and the final output is given as the softmax of two or three values (1, 2, or 3).

The above calculation computes the probabilities of the modification to candidate PUs, but it does so independently for each modifier PU; therefore, there may be crossing of modification in a whole sentence. Since the Japanese dependency structures are fully projective, the optimal tree for the sentence is constructed using a beam search to maximize the Equation (3) in Section 2.3, excluding modification pairs that violate the projective constraint in each step of the beam search. More specifically, combinations of dependencies which violate projective constraints (*e.g.* $5 \leftarrow 7$ and $6 \leftarrow 8$) are excluded from the beam, then the projective tree structure is guaranteed.

4 Experiments

4.1 Experimental settings

We used EDR Japanese Corpus (EDR, 1996) for the initial training and evaluation. After remov-

[4]Typical used as a topic marker, which suggests a long-distance dependency.

Training method	Training size	Accuracy	
nearest baseline	none	62.03%	(13581/21894)
logistic regression	190k	88.92%	(19468/21894)
NN	40k	88.15%	(19300/21894)
NN	80k	88.49%	(19373/21894)
NN	120k	89.17%	(19522/21894)
NN	160k	**89.31**%	(19554/21894)

Table 3: The accuracy of PU dependencies tested on EDR corpus. The 'nearest baseline' denotes the ratio of the case where the head is the right next PU.

ing inconsistent PUs due to tokenization mismatch between the corpus and the runtime process, the evaluation was conducted on 2,941 test sentences. 160,080 sentences were used for training and 8,829 sentences were kept for validation.

The models were implemented with TensorFlow (Abadi et al., 2015). The loss function was calculated by cross entropy. The L2 normalization factor multiplied by 10^{-8} was added, and output was optimized with AdamOptimizer (Kingma and Ba, 2014).

Words are expressed by two vectors. One was 100 dimensional embeddings of the surface form – the other was 50 dimensional embeddings of 148 types of values of the combination of 74 types of fine-grained PoS and a binary feature to find the existence of a comma in the PU. The three features between PUs were converted into 10 dimensional vectors. All of these vectors were randomly initialized and updated during the training. The input layer formed 990 in the triplet model and 1,320 dimensions in the quadruplet model. The dimension of the hidden layer was set to 200 and conducted a beam search with the size 5.

4.2 Experimental results

Table 3 shows the accuracies of dependency parsing by the conventional model trained with logistic regression and our proposed neural net model. Both models used the very similar grammar rules and the features are used. While the logistic regression method required manual selection of combination of features to get optimal accuracy, the neural net model outperformed the others when the training corpus was more than 120k sentences, by 0.4 points when the training corpus was 160k sentences. The maximum number of the training data in neural net model (160k) is less than that used in the logistic regression method (190k) because the development set needed to be kept for the neural model, and some sentences were dropped as described in Section 4.1.

Content words	Commas	Accuracy
Yes	Yes	**89.31**%
No	Yes	88.95%
Yes	No	87.40%
No	No	87.24%

Table 4: Ablation studies to remove content word vocabularies and commas.

Only words in the modifier PU and the candidate PUs were used in these methods, and other surrounding context and other dependencies were not considered. By capturing appropriate contexts of candidate PUs selected by the grammar rules and heuristics, our method successfully predicted the dependencies with relatively small pieces of information compared to the initial transition-based neural parser (Chen and Manning, 2014) that used a maximum of 18 words in the buffer, stack and modifiers.

There was a huge difference in the training speed. The logistic regression method took 4 to 20 hours on a CPU, but the neural net model converged in 5 to 15 seconds on a GPU.

We conducted an ablation study to see the contribution of attributes. We focused on the vocabulary of content words that can be better captured using distributed representation rather than the conventional method, and commas that played an important role in suggesting long-distance attachments. According to the results in Table 4, the contribution of the content words (the vocabulary size was 11,362) was not very big; even if the content words were ignored, the loss of accuracy was only 0.36 points. On the other hand, the model ignoring commas (where all of the features regarding commas was removed) downgraded the

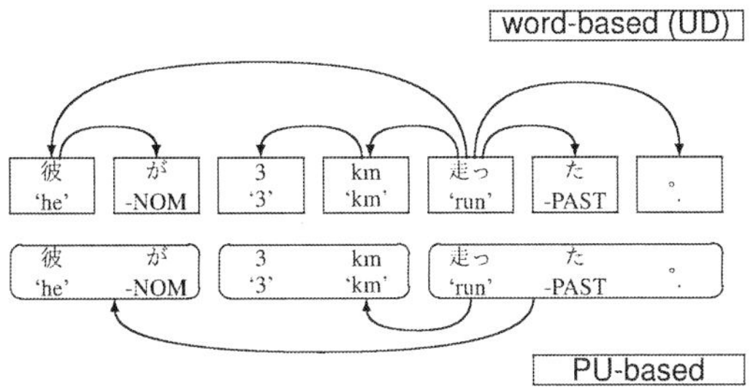

Figure 4: Conversion between PU-based and word-based dependencies.

accuracy by nearly 2 points, which suggests that commas are important in parsing.

The example dependency in Figure 3 ('president' ← 'introduced') was correctly solved by our neural model. Though many PUs followed the modifier PU in question, the model selected the head word from only three candidates restricted by the grammar rules, and the known dependency relationship between two PUs is guaranteed to be associated with the parsing result. The conventional model without neural net wrongly selected the first candidate ('acquired') as the head. The ablation of the content words also made the prediction wrong, that clarified that it was because the conventional model did not capture the content words and the attributes in the distance were stronger. On the other hand, the neural model with the content word embeddings appropriately captured the relationship between the functional word in the modifier PU (accusative case) and the content word of the correct candidate PU ('introduced').

4.3 Comparison on Japanese UD

To compare the performance of our parser with the results in the 2017 Shared Task (Zeman et al., 2017), we apply the trained model to UD Japanese-GSD [5] test data. As shown in Figure 4, the word-based dependency in UD Japanese and PU-based dependencies are interchangeable with a strict rule to detect PU boundaries and the head word in a PU. In UD Japanese-GSD data, the attachment direction between head words in PUs is always the same after converting to the PU-based structure. Also the non-head words in a PU always depends on the head word of the PU.

The first section of Table 5 shows comparisons with the shared task results. Here we evaluate them by UAS (unlabeled attachment score) rather than by LAS (labeled attachment score) because most of the Japanese labels can be deterministically assigned with the combination of the head and the dependent, and assignment with the rules can reproduce the labels in UD Japanese-GSD corpus, thus it is not fair to compare LAS with other machine learning methods. The scores are associated with tokenization accuracies because they highly affect Japanese parsing accuracies in the shared task to handle raw text inputs. Our model performed better than any other results in the shared task, though the comparison is not completely fair since we rely on the segmentation and functional word attachment based on the consistent rules with the UD data creation.

In the 2017 Shared Task, the raw text was used as the input, thus the performance of sentence splitting and tokenization highly affected the parsing result.[6] To make more direct comparisons in parsing, our results were mapped with the baseline tokenzation by UDPipe (Straka et al., 2016) which many task participants have used. That is, the parsing score was intentionally downgraded, but it outperformed any other results which used UDPipe tokenization as it was, as shown in the second section of Table 5.

Also we compared our parser when the gold tokens are given, with UDPipe UDv2.0 model (Straka and Straková, 2017), and RBG Parser (Lei et al., 2014) which was trained with UD Japanese-GSD training set. Our model had 9% and 20% less errors than UDPipe and RBG Parser, respectively.

5 Application to other languages

Our approach relies on the head-final feature of the languages. In addition to Japanese, Korean and Tamil are categorized as rigid head-final languages (Polinsky, 2012). Table 6 shows the ratio of head-final dependencies by languages in the Universal Dependencies version 2.0 development data. Though the word-level dependencies in UD do not reflect the head finalness as only 45% of Japanese dependencies have the head in the right side, but when it comes to content words (the list of functional PoSs are shown in the caption of Table 6) without functional labels and exceptional labels such as conjunction (see the caption again),

[5] It was formerly known as UD Japanese until 2017.

[6] The mismatched tokens are always regarded as parsing errors in the calculation of UAS/LAS.

	Models	Tokens	UAS
Own tokenizers	Our model	98.61	**94.03**
	TRL (Kanayama et al., 2017)	98.59	91.14
	HIT-SCIR (Che et al., 2017)	92.95	81.94
UDPipe default tokenization	Our model - UDPipe aligned	89.41	**75.88**
	C2L2 (Shi et al., 2017)	89.68	75.46
	Stanford (Dozat et al., 2017)	89.68	75.42
Gold tokenization	Our model - with gold tokenization	100.0	**95.97**
	UDPipe UDv2.0 model (Straka and Straková, 2017)	100.0	95.48
	RBG Parser (Lei et al., 2014)	100.0	94.94

Table 5: F1 scores of tokenization and UAS on the UD Japanese-GSD test set. The top section shows the systems which used their own tokenizers. The second section is a comparison with the systems relying on the default settings of UDPipe, and the bottom section is the situation to ru parsers using the gold PoS as input.

language	all	content	selected
ar	0.31	0.09	0.09
cs	0.56	0.45	0.49
en	0.61	0.49	0.54
fi	0.57	0.54	0.60
ja	0.45	0.96	**1.00**
he	0.48	0.21	0.21
hi	0.58	0.91	0.95
hu	0.69	0.72	0.76
id	0.36	0.24	0.30
kk	0.59	0.77	0.82
ko	0.63	0.70	**0.98**
ro	0.47	0.26	0.30
ru	0.49	0.39	0.43
ta	0.71	0.92	**0.97**
tr	0.64	0.78	0.87
ur	0.59	0.89	0.94
vi	0.41	0.34	0.36
zh	0.72	0.79	0.83

Table 6: The ratio of head-final dependencies by languages. "All" denotes the ratio of all nodes except for the root. "Content" is the head-final ratio for content words, *i.e.* functional PoSs (ADP, AUX, CCONJ, DET, SCONJ, SYM, PART, and PUNCT) are excluded. "selected" means the more selective ones, excluding the labels conj, fixed, flat, aux and mark.

Japanese has the complete head-final structures, and Korean and Tamil have high ratios supporting the linguistic theory.

However, the UD Korean corpus has so many coordination structures under the UD's general constraint that the left coordinate should be the head, because many subordinating structures are represented as coordination while corresponding Japanese ones are not, that it is difficult to convert the corpus to the strictly head-final structure. That is the reason why we could not evaluate our method on Korean, but the Triplet/Quadruplet Model has been applied to Korean with similar grammatical rules and it has been shown that the transfer learning from Japanese worked (Kanayama et al., 2014), thus our neural classifier approach to Korean parsing is expected to work well.

Also UD Tamil data has exceptional cases in proper nouns and other phenomena, and the relatively small corpus made the further investigation difficult. We are leaving it to future work.

6 Related work

The parsing approach to select heads of dependents has been proposed by Zhang et al. (2017). They applied bidirectional RNN to select the probability that each word chooses another word or the ROOT node as its head. They reported comparable results for four languages. Their method required a maximum spanning tree algorithm to generate valid trees. On the other hand, our approach straightforwardly outputs the projective tree by exploiting the head-final feature in Japanese.

Martínez-Alonso et al. (2017) shares the similar

motivation with ours. They tackled multilingual parsing by using a small set of attachment rules determined with Universal POS, and achieved 55 UAS value with predicted PoS as input. Our method applied a neural model on top of the grammatical restriction to achieve higher accuracy for a specific language.

García et al. (2017) tackled the multilingual shared task with the rule-based approach. The rules are simplified with the almost delexicalized PoS-level constraints and created with a small effort by an expert. Though the performance was limited compared to other supervised approaches, it is meaningful for the comparison of linguistic features, and the combination with machine learning methods can be useful as we are aiming at.

7 Conclusion

In this paper we implemented a neural net parsing model as the direct classifier to predict the attachment of phrasal units in a intuitive manner by exploiting grammatical knowledge and heuristics, and confirmed that the neural net model outperformed the conventional machine learning method, and our method worked better than the shared task results. Unlike the most of neural parsing methods in which interpretation of the model output and control of the model without data supervision are difficult, our method is simple enough to understand the behavior of the model, and the grammatical knowledge can be reflected in the restriction of modification candidates. Moreover, the neural net with distributed vector representations enabled us to handle more vocabularies than the logistic regression with distinct word features in which only the limited number of content words and their combination with other features could be distinguished in the parsing model.

Our experiments showed that a limited number of words are seen as able to predict attachments. For further improvement, we can integrate the LSTM model, which handles more contextual information with simplification (Cross and Huang, 2016). We did not handle coordination relationships explicitly in this work, but we will intend to address coordination with more lexical knowledge and a broader context.

References

Martín Abadi, Ashish Agarwal, Paul Barham, Eugene Brevdo, Zhifeng Chen, Craig Citro, Greg S. Corrado, Andy Davis, Jeffrey Dean, Matthieu Devin, Sanjay Ghemawat, Ian Goodfellow, Andrew Harp, Geoffrey Irving, Michael Isard, Yangqing Jia, Rafal Jozefowicz, Lukasz Kaiser, Manjunath Kudlur, Josh Levenberg, Dan Mané, Rajat Monga, Sherry Moore, Derek Murray, Chris Olah, Mike Schuster, Jonathon Shlens, Benoit Steiner, Ilya Sutskever, Kunal Talwar, Paul Tucker, Vincent Vanhoucke, Vijay Vasudevan, Fernanda Viégas, Oriol Vinyals, Pete Warden, Martin Wattenberg, Martin Wicke, Yuan Yu, and Xiaoqiang Zheng. 2015. TensorFlow: Large-scale machine learning on heterogeneous systems. Software available from tensorflow.org.

Masayuki Asahara, Hiroshi Kanayama, Takaaki Tanaka, Yusuke Miyao, Sumire Uematsu, Shinsuke Mori, Yuji Matsumoto, Mai Omura, and Yugo Murawaki. 2018. Universal Dependencies version 2 for Japanese. In *Proceedings of LREC 2018*.

Wanxiang Che, Jiang Guo, Yuxuan Wang, Bo Zheng, Huaipeng Zhao, Yang Liu, Dechuan Teng, and Ting Liu. 2017. The hit-scir system for end-to-end parsing of universal dependencies. *Proceedings of the CoNLL 2017 Shared Task: Multilingual Parsing from Raw Text to Universal Dependencies* pages 52–62.

Danqi Chen and Christopher Manning. 2014. A fast and accurate dependency parser using neural networks. In *Proceedings of the 2014 conference on empirical methods in natural language processing (EMNLP)*. pages 740–750.

James Cross and Liang Huang. 2016. Incremental parsing with minimal features using bi-directional lstm. In *The 54th Annual Meeting of the Association for Computational Linguistics*. page 32.

Timothy Dozat, Peng Qi, and Christopher D Manning. 2017. Stanford's graph-based neural dependency parser at the conll 2017 shared task. *Proceedings of the CoNLL 2017 Shared Task: Multilingual Parsing from Raw Text to Universal Dependencies* pages 20–30.

EDR. 1996. EDR (Japan Electronic Dictionary Research Institute, Ltd.) electronic dictionary version 1.5 technical guide.

Marcos García and Pablo Gamallo. 2017. A rule-based system for cross-lingual parsing of romance languages with universal dependencies. In *CoNLL Shared Task*.

Hiroshi Kanayama, Masayasu Muraoka, and Katsumasa Yoshikawa. 2017. A semi-universal pipelined approach to the conll 2017 ud shared task. *Proceedings of the CoNLL 2017 Shared Task: Multilingual Parsing from Raw Text to Universal Dependencies* pages 265–273.

Hiroshi Kanayama, Tetsuya Nasukawa, and Hideo Watanabe. 2004. Deeper sentiment analysis using machine translation technology. In *COLING 2004*. pages 494–500.

Hiroshi Kanayama, Youngja Park, Yuta Tsuboi, and Dongmook Yi. 2014. Learning from a neighbor: Adapting a japanese parser for korean through feature transfer learning. In *Proceedings of the EMNLP'2014 Workshop on Language Technology for Closely Related Languages and Language Variants*. pages 2–12.

Hiroshi Kanayama, Kentaro Torisawa, Yutaka Mitsuishi, and Jun'ichi Tsujii. 2000. A hybrid Japanese parser with hand-crafted grammar and statistics. In *Proceedings of the 18th International Conference on Computational Linguistics*. pages 411–417.

Daisuke Kawahara, Sadao Kurohashi, and Kôiti Hasida. 2002. Construction of a japanese relevance-tagged corpus. In *LREC*.

Diederik Kingma and Jimmy Ba. 2014. Adam: A method for stochastic optimization. *arXiv preprint arXiv:1412.6980*.

Tao Lei, Yuan Zhang, Regina Barzilay, and Tommi Jaakkola. 2014. Low-rank tensors for scoring dependency structures. Association for Computational Linguistics.

Héctor Martínez Alonso, Željko Agić, Barbara Plank, and Anders Søgaard. 2017. Parsing universal dependencies without training. In *Proceedings of the 15th Conference of the European Chapter of the Association for Computational Linguistics*. Valencia, Spain, pages 230–240.

Ryan McDonald, Fernando Pereira, Kiril Ribarov, and Jan Hajič. 2005. Non-projective dependency parsing using spanning tree algorithms. In *Proceedings of the conference on Human Language Technology and Empirical Methods in Natural Language Processing*. Association for Computational Linguistics, pages 523–530.

Tetsuya Nasukawa and Tohru Nagano. 2001. Text analysis and knowledge mining system. *IBM systems journal* 40(4):967–984.

Joakim Nivre, Cristina Bosco, Jinho Choi, Marie-Catherine de Marneffe, Timothy Dozat, Richard Farkas, Jennifer Foster, Filip Ginter, Yoav Goldberg, Jan Haji, Jenna Kanerva, Veronika Laippala, Alessandro Lenci, Teresa Lynn, Christopher Manning, Ryan McDonald, Anna Missila, Simonetta Montemagni, Slav Petrov, Sampo Pyysalo, Natalia Silveira, Maria Simi, Aaron Smith, Reut Tsarfaty, Veronika Vincze, and Daniel Zeman. 2015. Universal dependencies 1.0.

Joakim Nivre, Johan Hall, Jens Nilsson, Atanas Chanev, Gülşen Eryigit, Sandra Kübler, Svetoslav Marinov, and Erwin Marsi. 2007. Maltparser: A language-independent system for data-driven dependency parsing. *Natural Language Engineering* 13(2):95–135.

Joakim Nivre and Ryan McDonald. 2008. Integrating graph-based and transition-based dependency parsers. *Proceedings of ACL-08* pages 950–958.

Maria Polinsky. 2012. Headness, again. *UCLA Working Papers in Linguistics, Theories of Everything* 17:348–359.

Tianze Shi, Felix G Wu, Xilun Chen, and Yao Cheng. 2017. Combining global models for parsing universal dependencies. *Proceedings of the CoNLL 2017 Shared Task: Multilingual Parsing from Raw Text to Universal Dependencies* pages 31–39.

Milan Straka, Jan Hajic, and Jana Straková. 2016. Udpipe: Trainable pipeline for processing conll-u files performing tokenization, morphological analysis, pos tagging and parsing. In *LREC*.

Milan Straka and Jana Straková. 2017. Tokenizing, pos tagging, lemmatizing and parsing ud 2.0 with udpipe. In *Proceedings of the CoNLL 2017 Shared Task: Multilingual Parsing from Raw Text to Universal Dependencies*. Association for Computational Linguistics, pages 88–99.

Takaaki Tanaka, Yusuke Miyao, Masayuki Asahara, Sumire Uematsu, Hiroshi Kanayama, Shinsuke Mori, and Yuji Matsumoto. 2016. Universal dependencies for japanese. In *Proceedings of LREC 2016*.

Daniel Zeman, Martin Popel, Milan Straka, Jan Hajič, Joakim Nivre, Filip Ginter, Juhani Luotolahti, Sampo Pyysalo, Slav Petrov, Martin Potthast, Francis Tyers, Elena Badmaeva, Memduh Gökırmak, Anna Nedoluzhko, Silvie Cinková, Jan Hajič jr., Jaroslava Hlaváčová, Václava Kettnerová, Zdeňka Urešová, Jenna Kanerva, Stina Ojala, Anna Missilä, Christopher Manning, Sebastian Schuster, Siva Reddy, Dima Taji, Nizar Habash, Herman Leung, Marie-Catherine de Marneffe, Manuela Sanguinetti, Maria Simi, Hiroshi Kanayama, Valeria de Paiva, Kira Droganova, Hěctor Martínez Alonso, Hans Uszkoreit, Vivien Macketanz, Aljoscha Burchardt, Kim Harris, Katrin Marheinecke, Georg Rehm, Tolga Kayadelen, Mohammed Attia, Ali Elkahky, Zhuoran Yu, Emily Pitler, Saran Lertpradit, Michael Mandl, Jesse Kirchner, Hector Fernandez Alcalde, Jana Strnadova, Esha Banerjee, Ruli Manurung, Antonio Stella, Atsuko Shimada, Sookyoung Kwak, Gustavo Mendonça, Tatiana Lando, Rattima Nitisaroj, and Josie Li. 2017. CoNLL 2017 Shared Task: Multilingual Parsing from Raw Text to Universal Dependencies. In *Proceedings of the CoNLL 2017 Shared Task: Multilingual Parsing from Raw Text to Universal Dependencies*. Association for Computational Linguistics.

Xingxing Zhang, Jianpeng Cheng, and Mirella Lapata. 2017. Dependency parsing as head selection. In *Proceedings of the 15th Conference of the European Chapter of the Association for Computational Linguistics*. pages 665–676.

Syntactic Dependency Representations in Neural Relation Classification

Farhad Nooralahzadeh and **Lilja Øvrelid**
University of Oslo
Department of Informatics
{farhadno, liljao}@ifi.uio.no

Abstract

We investigate the use of different syntactic dependency representations in a neural relation classification task and compare the CoNLL, Stanford Basic and Universal Dependencies schemes. We further compare with a syntax-agnostic approach and perform an error analysis in order to gain a better understanding of the results.

1 Introduction

The neural advances in the field of NLP challenge long held assumptions regarding system architectures. The classical NLP systems, where components of increasing complexity are combined in a pipeline architecture are being challenged by end-to-end architectures that are trained on distributed word representations to directly produce different types of analyses traditionally assigned to downstream tasks. Syntactic parsing has been viewed as a crucial component for many tasks aimed at extracting various aspects of meaning from text, but recent work challenges many of these assumptions. For the task of semantic role labeling for instance, systems that make little or no use of syntactic information, have achieved state-of-the-art results (Marcheggiani et al., 2017). For tasks where syntactic information is still viewed as useful, a variety of new methods for the incorporation of syntactic information are employed, such as recursive models over parse trees (Socher et al., 2013; Ebrahimi and Dou, 2015) , tree-structured attention mechanisms (Kokkinos and Potamianos, 2017), multi-task learning (Wu et al., 2017), or the use of various types of syntactically aware input representations, such as embeddings over syntactic dependency paths (Xu et al., 2015b).

Dependency representations have by now become widely used representations for syntactic analysis, often motivated by their usefulness in

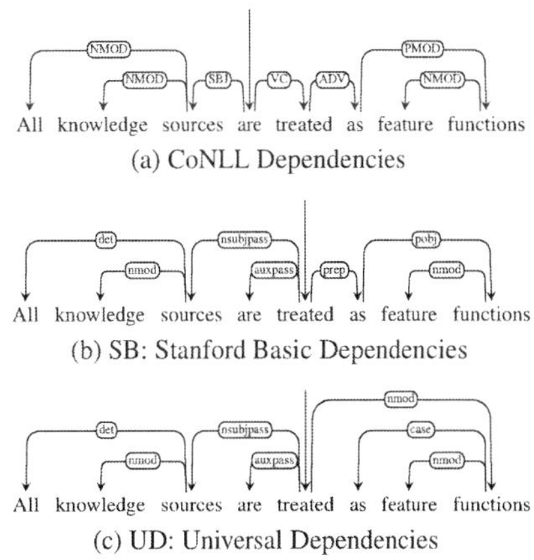

Figure 1: Dependency representations for the example sentence.

downstream application. There is currently a wide range of different types of dependency representations in use, which vary mainly in terms of choices concerning syntactic head status. Some previous studies have examined the effects of dependency representations in various downstream applications (Miyao et al., 2008; Elming et al., 2013). Most recently, the Shared Task on Extrinsic Parser Evaluation (Oepen et al., 2017) was aimed at providing better estimates of the relative utility of different types of dependency representations and syntactic parsers for downstream applications. The downstream systems in this previous work have, however, been limited to traditional (non-neural) systems and there is still a need for a better understanding of the contribution of syntactic information in neural downstream systems.

In this paper, we examine the use of syntactic representations in a neural approach to the task of relation classification. We quantify the effect of syntax by comparing to a syntax-agnostic approach and further compare different syntactic dependency representations that are used to generate embeddings over dependency paths.

Proceedings of the Workshop on the Relevance of Linguistic Structure in Neural Architectures for NLP, pages 47–53
Melbourne, Australia, July 19, 2018.

2 Dependency representations

Figure 1 illustrates the three different dependency representations we compare: the so-called CoNLL-style dependencies (Johansson and Nugues, 2007) which were used for the 2007, 2008, and 2009 shared tasks of the Conference on Natural Language Learning (CoNLL), the Stanford 'basic' dependencies (SB) (Marneffe et al., 2006) and the Universal Dependencies (v1.3) (UD; McDonald et al., 2013; Marneffe et al., 2014; Nivre et al., 2016). We see that the analyses differ both in terms of their choices of heads vs. dependents and the inventory of dependency types. Where CoNLL analyses tend to view functional words as heads (e.g., the auxiliary verb *are*), the Stanford scheme capitalizes more on content words as heads (e.g., the main verb *treated*). UD takes the tendency to select contentful heads one step further, analyzing the prepositional complement *functions* as a head, with the preposition *as* itself as a dependent case marker. This is in contrast to the CoNLL and Stanford scheme, where the preposition is head.

For syntactic parsing we employ the parser described in Bohnet and Nivre (2012), a transition-based parser which performs joint PoS-tagging and parsing. We train the parser on the standard training sections 02-21 of the Wall Street Journal (WSJ) portion of the Penn Treebank (Marcus et al., 1993). The constituency-based treebank is converted to dependencies using two different conversion tools: (i) the pennconverter software[1] (Johansson and Nugues, 2007), which produces the CoNLL dependencies[2], and (ii) the Stanford parser using either the option to produce basic dependencies [3] or its default option which is Universal Dependencies v1.3[4]. The parser achieves a labeled accuracy score of 91.23 when trained on the CoNLL08 representation, 91.31 for the Stanford basic model and 90.81 for the UD representation, when evaluated against the standard evaluation set (section 23) of the WSJ. We acknowledge that these results are not state-of-the-art parse results for English, however, the parser is straightforward to use and re-train with the different dependency representations. We also compare to another widely used parser, namely the pre-trained parsing model for English included in the Stanford CoreNLP toolkit (Manning et al., 2014), which outputs Universal Dependencies only. However, it was clearly outperformed by our version of the Bohnet and Nivre (2012) parser in the initial development experiments.

3 Relation extraction system

We evaluate the relative utility of different types of dependency representations on the task of semantic relation extraction and classification in scientific papers, SemEval Task 7 (Gábor et al., 2018). We make use of the system of Nooralahzadeh et al. (2018): a CNN classifier with dependency paths as input, which ranked 3rd (out of 28) participants in the overall evaluation of the shared task. Here, the shortest dependency path (*sdp*) connecting two target entities for each relation instance is provided by the parser and is embedded in the first layer of a CNN. We extend on their system by (i) implementing a syntax-agnostic approach, (ii) implementing hyper-parameter tuning for each dependency representation, and (iii) adding Universal Dependencies as input representation. We thus train classifiers with *sdps* extracted from the different dependency representations discussed above and measure the effect of this information by the performance of the classifier.

3.1 Dataset and Evaluation Metrics

We use the SemEval-2018, Task 7 dataset (Gábor et al., 2018) from its *Subtask 1.1*. The training data contains abstracts of 350 papers from the ACL Anthology Corpus, annotated for concepts and semantic relations. Given an abstract of a scientific paper with pre-annotated domain concepts, the task is to perform relation classification. The classification sub-task 1.1 contains 1228 entity pairs that are annotated based on five asymmetric relations (USAGE, RESULT, MODEL-FEATURE, PART_WHOLE, TOPIC) and one symmetric relation (COMPARE). The relation instance along with its directionality are provided in both the training and the test data sets. The official evaluation metric is the macro-averaged F1-scores for the six semantic relations, therefore we will compare the impact of different dependency representations on the macro-averaged F1-scores.

[1] `http://nlp.cs.lth.se/software/treebank-converter/`

[2] The pennconverter tool is run using the `rightBranching=false` flag.

[3] The Stanford parser is run using the `-basic` flag to produce the basic version of Stanford dependencies.

[4] Note, however, that the Stanford converter does not produce UD PoS-tags, but outputs native PTB tags.

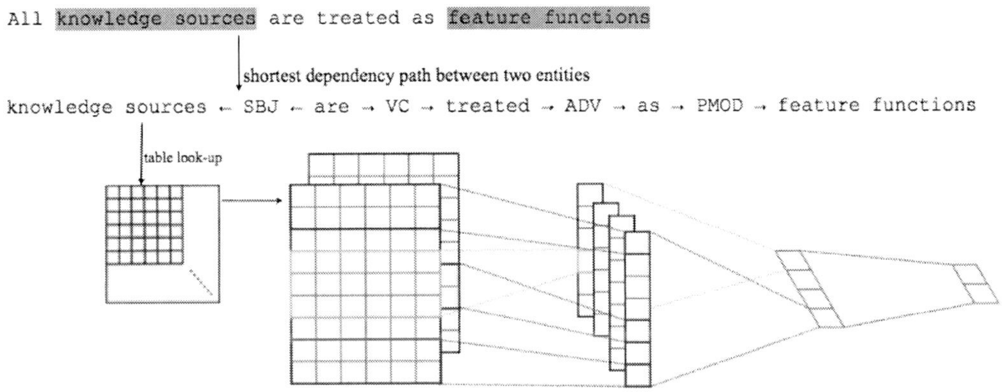

Figure 2: Model architecture with two channels for an example shortest dependency path (CNN model from Kim (2014)).

The training set for Subtask 1.1 is quite small, which is a challenge for end-to-end neural methods. To overcome this, we combined the provided datasets for Subtask 1.1 and Subtask 1.2 (relation classification on noisy data), which provides additional 350 abstracts and 1248 labeled entity pairs to train our model. This yields a positive impact (+16.00% F1) on the classification task in our initial experiments.

3.2 Pre-processing

Sentence and token boundaries are detected using the Stanford CoreNLP tool (Manning et al., 2014). Since most of the entities are multi-word units, we replace the entities with their codes in order to obtain a precise dependency path. Our example sentence *All knowledge sources are treated as feature functions*, an example of the USAGE relation between the two entities *knowledge sources* and *feature functions*, is thus transformed to `All P05_1057_3 are treated as P05_1057_4`.

Given an encoded sentence, we find the *sdp* connecting two target entities for each relation instance using a syntactic parser. Based on the dependency graph output by the parser, we extract the shortest dependency path connecting two entities. The path records the direction of arc traversal using left and right arrows (i.e. $\leftarrow$ and $\rightarrow$) as well as the dependency relation of the traversed arcs and the predicates involved, following Xu et al. (2015a). The entity codes in the final *sdp* are replaced with the corresponding word tokens at the end of the pre-processing step.

For the sentence above, we thus extract the path: `knowledge sources ← SBJ ← are → VC → treated → ADV → as → PMOD → feature functions`

3.3 CNN model

The system is based on a CNN architecture similar to the one used for sentence classification in Kim (2014). Figure 2 provides an overview of the proposed model. It consists of 4 main layers as follows: 1) **Look-up Table and Embedding layer:** In the first step, the model takes a shortest dependency path (i.e., the words, dependency edge directions and dependency labels) between entity pairs as input and maps it into a feature vector using a look-up table operation. Each element of the dependency path (i.e. word, dependency label and arrow) is transformed into a embedding layer by looking up the embedding matrix $M \in \mathcal{R}^{d \times V}$, where d is the dimension of CNN embedding layer and V is the size of vocabulary. Each column in the embedding matrix can be initialized randomly or with pre-trained embeddings. The dependency labels and edge directions are always initialized randomly. 2) **Convolutional Layer**: The next layer performs convolutions with ReLU activation over the embeddings using multiple filter sizes and extracts feature maps. 3) **Max pooling Layer**: By applying the *max* operator, the most effective local features are generated from each feature map. 4) **Fully connected Layer**: Finally, the higher level syntactic features are fed to a fully connected *softmax* layer which outputs the probability distribution over each relation.

Representation	Hyper parameters: Filter size	Num. Feature maps	Activation func.	L2 Reg.	Learning rate	Dropout Prob.	F1.(avg. in 5-fold): with default values	with optimal values
CoNLL08	4-5	1000	Softplus	1.15e+01	1.13e-03	1	73.34	74.49
SB	4-5	806	Sigmoid	8.13e-02	1.79e-03	0.87	72.83	**75.05**
UD v1.3	5	716	Softplus	1.66e+00	9.63E-04	1	68.93	69.57

Table 2: Hyper parameter optimization results for each model with different representation. The max pooling strategy consistently performs better in all model variations.

Relation	**best F1** (in 5-fold): without sdp	with sdp	**Diff.**
USAGE	60.34	80.24	+ 19.90
MODEL-FEATURE	48.89	70.00	+ 21.11
PART_WHOLE	29.51	70.27	+40.76
TOPIC	45.80	91.26	+45.46
RESULT	54.35	81.58	+27.23
COMPARE	20.00	61.82	+ 41.82
macro-averaged	50.10	76.10	+26.00

Table 1: Effect of using the shortest dependency path on each relation type.

4 Experiments

We run all the experiments with a multi-channel setting[5] in which the first channel is initialized with pre-trained embeddings [6] in static mode (i.e. it is not updated during training) and the second one is initialized randomly and is fine-tuned during training (non-static mode). The macro F1-score is measured by 5-fold cross validation and to deal with the effects of class imbalance, we weight the cost by the ratio of class instances, thus each observation receives a weight, depending on the class it belongs to.

4.1 Effect of syntactic information

To evaluate the effects of syntactic information in general for the relation classification task, we compare the performance of the model with and without the dependency paths. In the syntax-agnostic setup, a sentence that contains the participant entities is used as input for the CNN. We keep the value of hyper-parameters equal to the ones that are reported in the original work (Kim, 2014). To provide the *sdp* for the syntax-aware version we compare to, we use our parser with Stanford dependencies. We find that the effect of syntactic structure varies between the different relation types. However, the *sdp* information has a clear positive impact on all the relation types (Table 1). It can be attributed to the fact that the context-based representations suffer from irrelevant sub-sequences or clauses when target entities occur far from each other or there are other target entities in the same sentence. The *sdp* between two entities in the dependency graph captures a condensed representation of the information required to assert a relationship between two entities (Bunescu and Mooney, 2005).

4.2 Comparison of different dependency representations

To investigate the model performance with various parser representations, we create a *sdp* for each training example using the different parse models and exploit them as input to the relation classification model. With the use of default parameters there is a chance that these favour one of the representations. In order to perform a fair comparison, we make use of Bayesian optimization (Brochu et al., 2010) in order to locate optimal hyper parameters for each of the dependency representations. We construct a Bayesian optimization procedure using a Gaussian process with 100 iterations and Expected Improvement (EI) for its acquisition functions. We set the objective function to maximize the macro F1 score over 5-fold cross validation on the training set. Here we investigate the impact of various system design choices with the following parameters: [7]: I) Filter region size: $\in \{3, 4, 5, 6, 7, 8, 9, 3\text{-}4, 4\text{-}5, 5\text{-}6, 6\text{-}7, 7\text{-}8, 8\text{-}9, 3\text{-}4\text{-}5, 4\text{-}5\text{-}6, 5\text{-}6\text{-}7, 6\text{-}7\text{-}8, 7\text{-}8\text{-}9\}$ II) Number of feature maps for each filter region size: $\in \{10 : 1000\}$ III) Activation function: $\in \{Sigmoid, ReLU, Tanh, Softplus, Iden\}$. IV) Pooling strategy: $\in \{max, avg\}$. V) L2 regular-

[5]Initial experiments show that the multi-channel model works better than the single channel model

[6]We train 300-d domain-specific embeddings on the ACL Anthology corpus using the available word2vec implementation *gensim* for training.

[7]Default values are {3-4-5, 128, ReLU, max, 3, 1e-3, 0.5}

Sentence	This indicates that there is no need to add **punctuation** in transcribing **spoken corpora** simply in order to help parsers.	class: PART_WHOLE
CoNLL08	punctuation ← obj ← add → adv → in → pmod → transcribing → obj → spoken corpora	
SB	punctuation ← dobj ← add → prep → in → pcomp → transcribing → dobj → spoken corpora	
UD v1.3	punctuation ← dobj ← add → advcl → transcribing → dobj → spoken corpora	
Sentence	In the process we also provide a **formal definition** of **parsing** motivated by an informal notion due to Lang .	class: MODEL-FEATURE
CoNLL08	formal definition → nmod → of → pmod → parsing	
SB	formal definition → prep → of → pobj → parsing	
UD v1.3	formal definition → nmod → parsing	
Sentence	This paper describes a practical **"black-box" methodology** for automatic evaluation of **question-answering NL systems** in spoken dialogue.	class: USAGE
CoNLL	" "black-box" methodology → nmod → for → pmod → evaluation → nmod → of → pmod → question-answering NL systems	
SB	"black-box" methodology → prep → for → pobj → evaluation → prep → of → pobj → question-answering NL systems	
UD v1.3	"black-box" methodology → nmod → evaluation → nmod → question-answering NL systems	

Table 4: The examples for which the CoNLL/SB-based models correctly predict the relation type in 5-fold trials, whereas the UD based model has an incorrect prediction.

ization: $\in \{1e-4 : 1e+2\}$. VI) Learning rate: $\in \{1e-6 : 1e-2\}$. VII) Dropout probability [8]: $\in \{0.1 : 1\}$. Table 2 presents the optimal values for each configuration using different dependency representations. We see that the optimized parameter settings vary for the different representations, showing the importance of tuning for these types of comparisons. The results furthermore show that the *sdps* based on the Stanford Basic (SB) representation provide the best performance, followed by the CoNLL08 representation. We observe that the results for the UD representation are quite a bit lower than the two others.

5 Error analysis

Table 3 presents the effect of each parser representation in the classification task, broken down by relation type. We find that the UD-based model falls behind the others on the most relation types (i.e, COMPARE, MODEL-FEATURE, PART_WHOLE, TOPICS). To explore these differences in more detail, we manually inspect the instances for which the CoNLL/SB-based models correctly predict the re lation type in 5-fold trials, whereas the UD-based model has an incorrect prediction. Table 4 shows some of these examples, marking the entities and the gold class of each instance and also showing the *sdp* from each representation. We observe that the UD paths are generally shorter. A striking similarity between most of the instances is the fact that one of the entities resides in a prepositional phrase. Whereas the SB and CoNLL paths explicitly represent the preposition in the path, the UD representation does not. Clearly, the difference between for

[8]The probability that each element is kept, in which 1 implies that none of the nodes are dropped out

		best F1 (in 5-fold)		
Relation	**Frq.**	CoNLL	SB	UD
USAGE	947	76.84	82.39	77.56
MODEL-FEATURE	498	68.27	68.54	66.36
PART_WHOLE	425	75.32	71.28	67.11
TOPIC	258	89.32	90.57	87.62
RESULT	193	82.35	81.69	82.86
COMPARE	136	66.67	66.67	54.24
macro-averaged		76.94	77.57	72.83

Table 3: Effect of using the different parser representation on each relation type.

instance the USAGE and PART_WHOLE relation may be indicated by the presence of a specific preposition (*X for Y* vs. *X of Y*). This is also interesting since this particular syntactic choice has been shown in previous work to have a negative effect on intrinsic parsing results for English (Schwartz et al., 2012).

6 Conclusion

This paper has examined the use of dependency representations for neural relation classification and has compared three widely used representations. We find that representation matters and that certain choices have clear consequences in downstream processing. Future work will extend the study to neural dependency parsers and other relation classification data sets.

References

Bernd Bohnet and Joakim Nivre. 2012. A transition-based system for joint part-of-speech tagging and labeled non-projective dependency parsing. In *Proceedings of EMNLP*, pages 1455–1465, Jeju Island, Korea. ACL.

Eric Brochu, Vlad M. Cora, and Nando de Freitas. 2010. A tutorial on bayesian optimization of expensive cost functions, with application to active user modeling and hierarchical reinforcement learning. *CoRR*, abs/1012.2599.

Razvan C. Bunescu and Raymond J. Mooney. 2005. A shortest path dependency kernel for relation extraction. In *Proceedings of the Conference on Human Language Technology and Empirical Methods in Natural Language Processing*, HLT '05, pages 724–731, Stroudsburg, PA, USA. Association for Computational Linguistics.

Javid Ebrahimi and Dejing Dou. 2015. Chain based rnn for relation classification. In *HLT-NAACL*.

Jakob Elming, Anders Johannsen, Sigrid Klerke, Emanuele Lapponi, Héctor Martínez Alonso, and Anders Søgaard. 2013. Down-stream effects of tree-to-dependency conversions. In *Human Language Technologies: Conference of the North American Chapter of the Association of Computational Linguistics, 2013*, pages 617–626.

Kata Gábor, Davide Buscaldi, Anne-Kathrin Schumann, Behrang QasemiZadeh, Haïfa Zargayouna, and Thierry Charnois. 2018. Semeval-2018 Task 7: Semantic relation extraction and classification in scientific papers. In *Proceedings of International Workshop on Semantic Evaluation (SemEval-2018)*, New Orleans, LA, USA.

Richard Johansson and Pierre Nugues. 2007. Extended constituent-to-dependency conversion for english. In *NODALIDA 2007 Proceedings*, pages 105–112. University of Tartu.

Yoon Kim. 2014. Convolutional neural networks for sentence classification. In *Proceedings of the 2014 Conference on Empirical Methods in Natural Language Processing*, pages 1746–1751. Association for Computational Linguistics.

Filippos Kokkinos and Alexandros Potamianos. 2017. Structural attention neural networks for improved sentiment analysis. In *Meeting of the European Chapter of the Association for Computational Linguistics*, pages 586–591, Valencia, Spain.

Christopher D. Manning, Mihai Surdeanu, John Bauer, Jenny Finkel, Steven J. Bethard, and David McClosky. 2014. The Stanford CoreNLP natural language processing toolkit. In *Association for Computational Linguistics (ACL) System Demonstrations*, pages 55–60.

Diego Marcheggiani, Anton Frolov, and Ivan Titov. 2017. A simple and accurate syntax-agnostic neural model for dependency-based semantic role labeling. In *Proceedings of the 21st Conference on Computational Natural Language Learning*, pages 411–420. Association for Computational Linguistics.

Mitchell Marcus, Beatrice Santorini, and Mary Ann Marcinkiewicz. 1993. Building a large annotated corpora of English. The Penn Treebank. *Journal of Computational Linguistics*, 19:313–330.

M. Marneffe, B. Maccartney, and C. Manning. 2006. Generating typed dependency parses from phrase structure parses. In *Proceedings of the Fifth International Conference on Language Resources and Evaluation (LREC-2006)*.

Marie-Catherine de Marneffe, Timothy Dozat, Natalia Silveira, Katri Haverinen, Filip Ginter, Joakim Nivre, and Christopher D. Manning. 2014. Universal stanford dependencies: A cross-linguistic typology. In *Proceedings of the Ninth International Conference on Language Resources and Evaluation (LREC-2014)*.

Ryan McDonald, Joakim Nivre, Yvonne Quirmbach-Brundage, Yoav Goldberg, Dipanjan Das, Kuzman Ganchev, Keith Hall, Slav Petrov, Hao Zhang, and Oscar Täckström. 2013. Universal dependency annotation for multilingual parsing. In *Proceedings ofAssociation for Computational Linguistics (ACL)*, pages 92–97.

Yusuke Miyao, Rune Sætre, Kenji Sagae, Takuya Matsuzaki, and Jun'ichi Tsujii. 2008. Task-oriented evaluation of syntactic parsers and their representations. In *Meeting of the Association for Computational Linguistics*, pages 46–54, Columbus, OH, USA.

Joakim Nivre, Marie-Catherine de Marneffe, Filip Ginter, Yoav Goldberg, Jan Hajic, Christopher D. Manning, Ryan T. McDonald, Slav Petrov, Sampo Pyysalo, Natalia Silveira, Reut Tsarfaty, and Daniel Zeman. 2016. Universal dependencies v1: A multilingual treebank collection. In *Proceedings of the Tenth International Conference on Language Resources and Evaluation LREC*.

Farhad Nooralahzadeh, Lilja Øvrelid, and Jan Tore Lønning. 2018. Sirius-ltg-uio at semeval-2018 task 7: Convolutional neural networks with shortest dependency paths for semantic relation extraction and classification in scientific papers. In *Proceedings of the 12th International Workshop on Semantic Evaluation (SemEval-2018*, New Orleans, LA, USA.

Stephan Oepen, Lilja Øvrelid, Jari Björne, Richard Johansson, Emanuele Lapponi, Filip Ginter, and Erik Velldal. 2017. The 2017 Shared Task on Extrinsic Parser Evaluation. Towards a reusable community infrastructure. In *Proceedings of the 2017 Shared Task on Extrinsic Parser Evaluation at the Fourth International Conference on Dependency Linguistics and the 15th International Conference on Parsing Technologies*, pages 1–12, Pisa, Italy.

Roy Schwartz, Omri Abend, and Ari Rappoport. 2012. Learnability-based syntactic annotation design. In *Proceedings of COLING 2012*, pages 2405–2422. The COLING 2012 Organizing Committee.

Richard Socher, Alex Perelygin, Jean Wu, Jason Chuang, Chris Manning, Andrew Ng, and Chris Potts. 2013. Recursive deep models for semantic compositionality over a sentiment treebank. In *Conference on Empirical Methods in Natural Language Processing*, pages 1631–1642, Seattle, WA, USA.

Shuangzhi Wu, Dongdong Zhang, Nan Yang, Mu Li, and Ming Zhou. 2017. Sequence-to-dependency neural machine translation. In *Meeting of the Association for Computational Linguistics*, pages 698–707, Vancouver, Canada.

Kun Xu, Yansong Feng, Songfang Huang, and Dongyan Zhao. 2015a. Semantic relation classification via convolutional neural networks with simple negative sampling. *CoRR*, abs/1506.07650.

Yan Xu, Lili Mou, Ge Li, Yunchuan Chen, Hao Peng, and Zhi Jin. 2015b. Classifying relations via long short term memory networks along shortest dependency paths. In *Conference on Empirical Methods in Natural Language Processing*, pages 1785–1794, Lisbon, Portugal.

Author Index

Association for Computational Linguistics
209 N. Eighth Street
Stroudsburg, Pennsylvania 18360

ISBN 978-1-5108-6716-1

CURRAN ASSOCIATES INC.
proceedings.com